A Whole, A Fragment

A Whole, A Fragment

Kurt H. Wolff

LEXINGTON BOOKS
Lanham • Boulder • New York • Oxford

LEXINGTON BOOKS

Published in the United States of America
by Lexington Books
A Member of the Rowman & Littlefield Publishing Group
4720 Boston Way, Lanham, Maryland 20706

PO Box 317
Oxford
OX2 9RU, UK

Copyright © 2002 by Lexington Books

All rights reserved. No part of this publication may be reproduced, stored in a retrieval system, or transmitted in any form or by any means, electronic, mechanical, photocopying, recording, or otherwise, without the prior permission of the publisher.

British Library Cataloguing in Publication Information Available

Library of Congress Cataloging-in-Publication Data

Wolff, Kurt H., 1912-
    A whole, a fragment / Kurt H. Wolff.
        p. cm.
Includes bibliographical references and index.
    ISBN 0-7391-0390-3 (alk. paper)
    I. Title.
    PT2647.O574 W46 2002
    838' .91407—dc21
                                        2002006477

Printed in the United States of America

∞™ The paper used in this publication meets the minimum requirements of American National Standard for Information Sciences—Permanence of Paper for Printed Library Materials, ANSI/NISO Z39.48-1992.

Carla

May 17, 1905—April 10, 1990

Contents

Foreword		ix
Preface		xiii
Chapter 1	"I Know I Am Not Yet Ready"	1
Chapter 2	*Vorgang*	3
Chapter 3	Hannah Arendt and Hermann Broch	43
Chapter 4	Another Beginning	57
Chapter 5	To Loma	75
Chapter 6	Loma in the Nineties—Suddenly	93
Chapter 7	Suddenly—Suddenly and Thanks to Hans Mohr	103
Acknowledgments		117
Index		119
About the Author		127

Foreword

Kurt Wolff's *A Whole, A Fragment* is a rich and provocative work. Wolff's deep roots within the continental tradition are manifest here, in a book that is a significant contribution to phenomenology, existentialism, and hermeneutics. But this book will also make its contribution well outside the continental tradition, as a text in ethics, autobiography, and what might be called fieldwork in the life-world. Wolff introduces a playfulness and a study in humor that emerges at many points, echoing the chapter "A Structure to Play With," in his book *What It Contains*.

We also see in this book how his work on surrender-and-catch fits within that tradition, as he discusses this notion—early in its formation—in correspondence with Hannah Arendt and Hermann Broch. Wolff's conception of surrender-and-catch has much to offer about human knowledge and the relation of epistemology to experience. Wolff has described surrender-and-catch as "cognitive love," entailing the suspension of prior beliefs and assumptions and entailing also an openness that makes it possible for the individual to grasp something to which he or she would not have been receptive otherwise.

It stands in stark contrast with the Enlightenment view of knowledge and of learning: that knowledge stands on its own, and anyone with senses and reason can access it. Surrender-and-catch obliges us to acknowledge our "locatedness," that we are always already located in a cultural, social, and biographical context and that the way out involves a radical suspension of our usual expectations and assumptions. Surrender-and-catch invites us to consider the possibility that learning means far more than acquiring new information within our current paradigm; indeed, learning means that we acquire far more than information, that we instead experience new dimensions of ourselves and our humanity.

While Wolff's own intellectual history owes much (and has contributed much) to sociology of knowledge, this book is perhaps foremost a work in phenomenology. As with his earlier work on Loma, Wolff presents a conception of fieldwork which goes well beyond the usual choices of empiricism and participant observation. Wolff's discussion of Loma and the conception of fieldwork it contains depict the texture of engagement as an extraordinary openness to being. In visiting a foreign place, we lose ourselves and become immersed in the rush of new sights and sounds. Each day seems endlessly long and rich, and the whole of our experience is immeasurably more acute than is the case in daily life, where we simply don't see large parts of our environment at all.

At the same time, Wolff invokes an existentialist perspective in the self-inquiry that this book contains and the junctures and moments of his life that he captures. Where existentialist writers such as Sartre state in fairly abstract terms that we are responsible for our natures and for the content of our lives, Wolff employs this notion concretely and in detail: He identifies and describes the self-construction of his life, not only in the ordinary sense of the decisions and regrets, but in a much fuller sense that captures the texture of our experience of living—dreams, ideas, and experiences revisited; the acute awareness of the body and the senses, of the objects of daily life, the texture of one's whole mental life; the contents, the pacing, the color, the movement from one sort of content to another and another. That is fully as much of what we construct when we construct our own lives as are the junctures when we choose a career or marry a spouse.

In much the same way that Wolff works phenomenologically, his notion of the "palimpsest" is a way of employing directly the fundamental notions of hermeneutics. Wolff returns to experiences, dreams, phrases, revisiting them each time from within another context. It strikes me that a structure he used several times in this volume lent itself particularly well to this: He begins by simply writing a piece, which often has the texture of a prose poem. I am thinking, for example, the section where he first says "With the cloth of shame I covered my face and passed on." He then thematizes particular phrases or sections, such as "With the cloth of shame I covered my face and passed on" and explores it more analytically. He revisits the phrase again at various points throughout the manuscript, each time looking at it from a new vantage point. His method is thoroughly hermeneutical; it seems to me that he is taking the insight of hermeneutics—that the meaning of an event, or text, is acquired and elaborated each time it is revisited from another perspective. But in the case of Wolff's book, he seems to be saying—or rather demonstrating—that this is also the process that characterizes all of our engagement with the world, as well as self-construction and our engagement with ourselves. There is also a kind of existentialist twist here as well: If Sartre would say that we are condemned to be free, Wolff would say that we are condemned to interpret as well, and that this interpretation is part and parcel of the self-construction, which is ineluctable. The letter from Arendt is telling in this regard; I am thinking in particular of Arendt's observation "And if you think about it, it is even harder to understand why you don't keep on writing at this piece, the Vorgang, until the end of your life. The only thing that stands against it would be life itself."

The discussion of surrender, birth, and the metaphor of drunkenness are striking as well, suggesting a move from continental methodologies to return to Plato's *Symposium*, with its elaborate plays on intoxication, seduction, and procreation. Whereas phenomenology, existentialism, and hermeneutics are deeply rooted in intellect, introspection, and metaphysical freedom, Wolff takes us again and again to the realms of passion and love and an experience of the world that is intoxicating and consuming. It seems to me that Wolff is invoking Plato's view that love, and the surrender that is implicit in it, carries us to some higher level of being, gives us access to an experience of reality that is unavailable without the surrender. In the end, it is a very different way into existentialism: If existentialism demands of us that we exert our will and determine our being, Wolff would have us achieve a greater integrity and authenticity by a very different route—not by imposing our will, but rather letting it go, to see what is there when we open ourselves to the world rather than imposing our wills upon it. I think that Broch captures this when he discusses Wolff's early work as a "rational poem" which seeks to bring about "a primordial relation between subject and object."

For those studying Sartre, Husserl, Merleau-Ponty, and Gadamer, *A Whole, A Fragment* provides a novel, insightful way of illustrating what these notions look like. For those interested in literary theory, it demonstrates an author's relation to the text as process rather than product. And for those interested in intellectual autobiography, it is a lyrical, elegant study.

Professor Joy Gordon

Preface

When I wrote this page I was in the midst of work on this book, but somehow I knew that this page should be, would be, the beginning of the book. It would bring out, right at the beginning, the fragmentary character the book would have, that the work would be composed of fragments, which nevertheless would make up a whole. The title of this book is to convey as much: *A Whole, A Fragment* means that the book is both: a whole consisting of fragments but itself a fragment consisting of fragments, some of which are wholes.

There is more in the book on wholes and fragments and their relations, an issue which has to do with my life, perhaps with human life, or, more likely, some human lives. But I must leave this with you, this book's reader, for which I thank you so much that you are.

CHAPTER 1

"I Know I Am Not Yet Ready"

I know I am not yet ready. What I have in mind is to start with *Vorgang*, allowing what comes then to come from my rereading of *Vorgang*. Unless this brings about changes, the next text is an analysis of Hannah Arendt's letter on *Vorgang*. I have written this analysis already but may have to make changes in light of what may have happened to my thoughts and thus to this text by then. What by now looks like the third part of this book is the attempt to understand my thus far inextinguishable attraction to *Vorgang* and to Loma, an experience only nine years later than the experience of *Vorgang*, and to uncover connections between the two. The reader should know that I follow where my thoughts and feelings lead, rather than a preset topic that must not be abandoned. This procedure is obvious to me but may be alienating to the reader in the two parts already written at this time, the analysis of Arendt's letter and that on the relations between *Vorgang* and Loma, and it is a characteristic of "surrender"; of surrender I know I will say more, but for the moment I can mark it as that attitude in which the person who would know suspends, as best he or she can and is willing to bear, as many received notions—concepts, rules, theories, postulates, etc.—as possible.

I think and have long thought that *Vorgang* and Loma are the most important experiences of my life. Until only recently, I asked myself how to account for the fact that I didn't think of Nazism as among my "most important experiences"—Nazism, which drove me out of my native country, hometown, house in which I was born and grew up, my own unforgettable room. It took me some time to be able to answer this question: Nazism didn't change me, it only changed my setting. I myself had to do what I had to do, whatever the changes in my life. I had a task or a mission—this will again come up much later in this book; in its articulation and development *Vorgang* and Loma were pivotal—as best I understand it, this task is the exploration of "surrender-and-catch" and its bearings and relations.

First, then, a translation of *Vorgang*. I discovered only quite recently that I had translated it in 1945, but not the longest part, "Interpretation"; ten years after writing *Vorgang*, then the original was the major piece in a collection of my earlier German writings.[1] I had been in this country only since 1939, and I shall now see how my English has improved, or so I hope.

Note

1. "Vorgang," in *Vorgang und immerwahrende Revolution* (Wiesbaden: Heymann, 1978), 3–49. Reprinted, with (later) drawings, in *Sozialwissenschaften als Kunst*, edited by Peter Ludes (Konstanz: Universitatsverlag, 1997), 139–87. These two books also contain Hannah Arendt's and Hermann Broch's comments on *Vorgang* and my letter to Broch.

CHAPTER 2

Vorgang

I can see the end of my checking the translation of *Vorgang*, and I can see myself commenting on *Vorgang*, thus fulfilling Hannah Arendt's suggestion of interpret and interpretation (see "Dreamland" later in this chapter). Not that I worry about all that is going to go into this writing; on this date, October 1, 1998, there is *Vorgang* in English, Hannah Arendt's letter, and my pages about it. And I know that what is still missing is the translation of Hermann Broch's commentary on *Vorgang* and my response to it, as well as a whole section on Loma.

I am still not quite done with the translation of *Vorgang* but I am eager to move the work forward. I find that my thoughts about this work, temporary and only on the way as they are, are part of it. I just uttered such a thought. I am again struck by the fact—or that is what I think it is—that this is rare in much contemporary writing in the social sciences. If so, it must be part of the desire for, and the tradition of, separating the author from his or her work, thus giving the work the appearance of objectivity, as if objectivity could be attained by neglecting origin. Instead, objectivity, it seems to me, has nothing to do with ignoring or silencing origin but, on the contrary, with facing origin and trying to identify its influence on one's work. (This does not apply to all intellectual and artistic work, including social sciences, but only to that which tries to develop thoughts. Enough, though, of these no more than preliminary remarks.)

No speaking or writing can do without concepts, but concepts cannot do justice to experience. Thus there is in the relation between concept and experience a parallel, probably much more than a parallel, with the "paradox of socialization": without socialization, which tells us how to meet the world, we would have no way of meeting it in any fashion; at the same time, we cannot meet it other than in a particular fashion which we have learned by socialization; thus the paradox of socialization results as our access to the world being limited to the choice between none and one-sided distortion. Similarly, concepts, that is, words, cannot do justice to experience (as Simmel, among others, has observed) but are the only means we have to describe and, above all, analyze experience. (Just as it is possible to reach reality without the interference of socialization, as in the experience of feelings, so it is possible to reach it by encountering art and thought, both of which are "out of this world," that is, the world into which we have been socialized.)

As far as I can make out, the connection between my enterprise here and the thoughts just hinted at is that both *Vorgang* and Loma are not only experiences that no conceptualization can do justice to, for this is true of all experiences. What is unique about *Vorgang* and Loma is their challenge: they don't let me rest until I have at least made some progress in understanding them, including an account of why it took so long to feel their importance.

Beginning

1

Face to face: there stands the word. Face to face the sea, separated from me by hardly three rooms, face to face with me that pure hall, the clarity of which makes me shiver and yet smiles at me, but I am swerving so that some words are determined by the swerve of the beautiful letter: did I not love the smoothness of the "R," it would perhaps not have come to "by three rooms," but in the drunkenness after all the swerve then really becomes the word, lust becomes validity, the very unique—the word which stands there against every reflection—readable. Reeling, lovingest seeing, seeing into the sea, above the sea: it clears wide under my window, reeling with which I am alone, with which alone I can be if I am myself.

Call on me, how should it not come out of the deepest wine jugs what in the years fermented in the sea and filled the drunkenness from which I was far away? Pour, I am holding the glass, deep, and it presses against all clarity of the sea, which begins at the mountain's spread and knows that the dark drink blesses the tides.

2
Drunkenness—but the rock that appears when the sea sinks back? Already the rock, but how much more crab- and snaildom ask what the drunkenness means, by what who is drunk and what is changed thereby? The meaning? But there I see, from the rock, a square with movement carriers that changes uncannily; I see the tender shell in the presoftened depth in its heavy night, how the green bulbous plants sway in the water wind—I am thinking of the word, more precisely, I remember having heard it, how does this go with the sense of a soft shell and fear of crabdom? I can't say it more generally, no word or concept meets it, what crab means to me is unique, is the crab feeling, shell feeling; so everything has a soul, and every point has its name in the heart, its heart name, named or not, heavy nightmare, the eyes close.

Thus there also is theory: what a difficult word, reachable only by means of equipments! To be sure, everything is theory, but who stepped back and gave it the name?

What is the idea of the last two paragraphs? What an idle, dangerous cover to call them theory! For everything is as it is, shell and word: a new sound.

3
There still is giving birth. If I look out on the sea, the rock-sprayed sea, stones ringed by the sea, the sky, ship and man rope—tied now more tightly, now more loosely; if I see on the little port square the girls seductively walking, the golden eyes playing green above the breasts and the hands around the laps, the baby already in their arms, the men dark trousers, laughing, already around the body; when I see the ice cream being sold, the cats playing on the walls, the old heavenly child, with lashed eyes, a fine nose and laughing mouth; when I see how the old man spits, how the ship is being equipped for the distant voyage with the nets to catch and how the wine covers, vaults, and suspends being in the strong blind image: I am still light and sore in my heart, light because it is and I find myself face to face: there stands the word; and sore because I am not it, light because everything comes out of me, sore because my mourning hangs around it.

4
And because I am still cringing with womb pain and uncertainty about the image of the birth which must still be described, for where would the tree be if we didn't say: this is it, and where the spirit if we didn't say: he has it? This somebody has called theory, but I feel and say: it is.

And as it becomes, we have it increasingly. For the wine is wonderful, the rock is blueing under the green sea, the sea is blueing under the green of the coast's fall! It is pale under the resounding tent and deep violet it shines up through the deep, deep cup. An embrace are rock and sea under the white sun, in the little room I sit with wine and pen in the finest noon above the sauntering sea. Flown away are Pan and the Fairies who never were, because I already will no more do with sounds, already it flies before my eyes, beslavered, hostile friend, the ear, I smell it, even in the fingers it slips already, all in labor, out of the port shoots the fishing boat, its mast already is at the horizon, distant, near only to itself, the boat just goes along with it, and the crew neighs with sea and bliss. Wine jar and water jar, table on which it writes, deep the sea, cursed, smooth, lovely one.

5

As if I hesitated! Like a boat in ecstasy, but it is still not wavy enough to scream with dance and trilling death. Death, come with your germ! Swallow flight, dizzy the air! Tears, choke the burden! Break out, my arms, with lust! Lust, my laughter, bribe murder and nourishment! Moment, fly up like a winged scythe, mow the world, my body is its shell, which drones and heaves, the world bloodbeat.

When I rest, how it smiles to you, fruits to you, morning, my carpet.

6

But now it is still noon, and wine and sun are strong and weak in the air. Will they let me? Does it seem so because I see them? Certainly, I am no longer choosy with voices and colors, it's closer. Thus, no what, no loss because drunkenness would appear less drunk, only: so it has gone, give me the hands full, the law.

These then are the first blows with the cold chisel: no matter how often I go over it, the sentence stands, clarified by the observation that this is the course of this writing. When we later enter more sober fields in which there is digging going on; when we—to imaging that landscape already—speak more abstractly, imagelessly, or—to name it from the present—we are simply different, is there a transition? Does the road lead not from Dionysus to Apollo but to the microscope, but how does he, and does he, remain the same? Up to now we can know only: what is here is for our condition the road, and for that later one it belongs to its knowledge. How the question lures!

7

What then—letting yourself glide into the sea, fructifier, sea-benumber—is knowing? The question. The question pregnant with answer, ornated with answer: it is the drunkenness which holds some other, the eye which shelters the other, the itching for the sake of scratching (I walk about scratching my flea bites, the fleas come from a dog who no longer is here): shudders of sickness and death as drunkenness, technique as life heightening, brain as stimulant: knowledge explains only at this stage, but drunk with ineluctability of being, this being, lifted up above the landscape from which the explanation grew, as being One like the pine (compared with the other as compared with the birch). Accordingly, since no longer valid only for the landscape, is the logos, our inner structure, which here ecstasy moves, everywhere? Where does the tie to the landscape end, where does the new sound begin? How is it that something not only is as it is but interpretable or even unambiguous?

My child! My child!

Let yourself be looked at, show yourself!

Interpretation

What does interpretation mean? Here: a look—a moment of rest. Since I write it so because it is so, because it must be so, it is justified, fear (what of?) has gone and full doing has been reached. (I can already say something explanatory: poetic work is easier, for the consciousness of doing, the question of what I am doing does not exist; here, however, it evidently is urgent.) On what then the glance? If I say that my writing is as it is, this does not mean fatalism as the words may well sound, that is, sound like an opinion come about by the constellation of diverse factors. For it is so as I make it because I have to, and also the despairs and doubts that I must go through because I am driven against them are because they are that way, because I am that way; and if I asked myself why I am that way, then even that question and its answer or attempts at answering would be the way they are because they must be so, and they must be so because I have made them so, and I have made them so because I had to make them so, and I had to make them so because I am I.

But the moment of rest urges me also to something else. That which will come must be as it will be, but how will it be? If I try, just to hold on to something, a picture (in order to recognize from its after all predictable falseness only the correct more clearly), e.g., of a house which is built without a plan, merely following the inspirations of the moment, to the second story but which now is being recognized as needing a third. One sees that something is missing, sees so to speak the missing before one's eyes, one feels that something should be there and asks, how must that be which must be here?—Is it so? But how do we come to relate such fundamentally different things, such independent things, to one another? Where is there something between house and letter or paper or me? But it is not that we compare the house, the particular house in this or that street or even when we stand before a new house and the comparison comes to us in view of this particular house, then we do not mean this one which is as it is in all its details, not to be confused with any other house whatsoever; what we mean is a house built up to the second floor but without the third, no matter whether built of brick or marble, whether provided with ornaments or not: actually we always have a vague image, probably according to whether we have grown up in Gdansk or Carrara, that we can copy from the unique houses just as these from that one and say: the house. This Plato has asked, and more: how come we have the idea of the house? And how the comparison is possible was what Kant asked and thought that because I myself make it, unity is possible and plausible.

And yet, our comparison is wrong. Admitting that its question is cleared, and the answer to the question of how a comparison is possible is given (which it isn't for me); here—and again, harmlessly, we are making a comparison—only a future place has resulted where it can go, here there only is some calming down; we are, remember, in the moment of rest; also recognizing the strange circumstance that the comparison, however just it may appear, asks what nevertheless is not correct about it? When it is after all the best possible comparison? It is wrong because the architect is one thing and the house something else, because the architect and the building material is different from me and the language, because the man there is building a house, but I am not building, and language is not material, but I present myself by means of language, in the language, it urges me, and I must just squirm that I just grasp it—it becomes as it becomes because I cannot be or do any other. But this is the full doing of the moment of rest, and the fear (of what?) is gone? Only drunkenness allows the justified comparison, but I am in the interpretation, on the way to another full doing—perhaps it will serve sometime to name what has just been done or has just been.

Still a last look: earlier (similar to how Plato and Kant strike me as more sleepwalking and I more awake) I wrote in situations like this one, which will at once be named: situation of all being—always "incomprehensibly" as the only possibility. Now I think: am I tired that I, surely without having grasped everything, simply go at the interpretation of the first part (in the hope that in its course I liberate its last sentence of its quotation marks which really belong there and were omitted only because of sloppiness if I cannot explain)? But this tiredness too is because it has to be, like everything else that there is for me to do and to suffer.

1

Interpretation! Let us be careful not to say that we now want to explicate what was implicated in the first part. Let us say, more simply and understandably (in this kind of expression we do stay in that of the first part itself) that the morning after the experience we want to reflect on it, see the transformations which yesterday's drunkenness has brought about, the foam out of our drunkenness. Or—and now we express ourselves in the manner of the following part which for the purposes of a preliminarily orienting cataloging we call scientific (without this word having any "definition" or a longer explanation that could be felt; but we think here, too, that we can later still contribute something) here we try to pick out the insights contained in the first part in order to clarify the method of that part, and to draw consequences that are not yet foreseeable in advance.

Strange expressions. But we are coming closer to an unreflected approach to the goal, interpretation, for if without further reflection I say, "strange," I am in a mood that imitates the first part, and when I previously talked scientifically, it was an impertinent, false anticipation of fields as yet unexplored. But all these words standing here also have their character and be it neither poetic nor scientific. This character appeared already in several places, which I want to remember, for later I will have to think of something like exploitation.

2

I want to do as best I can.

The drunkenness finally calmed down—with many heartbeats, with many glances, and yet having me myself, trusting, unconcerned with any interpretation of the beginning, for it was a beginning, and it also had a significance: there I wrote, at the capital F, the first letter, still staying in the moment of the anxiety of giving birth, but then swinging and with a swing setting down on paper the open curve, the words "face to face." In order to hold the cliff reached, but already feeling like climbing higher, always toward the view—for everything was still before me and I did not know to which place it went—I added: "there stands the word," a swinging, drunken beginning: "face to face the sea"—but "separated from me"? Well, I am sitting here in the third floor of a house, right above the Mediterranean, out of the window only the sea, perhaps only the sea, perhaps (actually most of the time) boats in view, rarely ships, the view that as a rule comprehends only the sea up to a certain line and above it the sky, a comfortable picture, simply in the window frame. But still distant, probably not only because of the measurable lines through the air, but, "by hardly three rooms," as if what was at issue were my house, with the sea belonging to it, "face to face with me that" pure hall, so to speak the architectonic jewel of purity and slightness of this apartment of drunkenness, namely, after all, "hardly" three rooms distant, magnificent property, what feeling of property ownership! How can I describe it to show it, to myself and my friends, my beloved figures, to present it graspably in its beauty? I can compare it only with "the purity of the R sound, "the 'R,'" but I don't know whether with this I have it all in its purity, simplicity, extension to an area, I'd say, "the clarity of which makes us shiver," but it is not strange to me, for it is my appropriate, correct, suitable apartment so that it "yet smiles at me." Let then yourself be held fast, the preconditions are good, the constellation is just, thus it is that I take courage, observe myself, "but I am swerving so that some words are determined by the swerve of the beautiful letter"; yet it is still something other than observation, it is also a moral-aesthetic emotion, an internal blushing—and by means of the adjective we are getting still closer to the lover, for he too presumably has the fleeting feeling that he must not now see the freckles on the dearest forehead, but is glad with his eyes which take also the reddish spots into the drunkenness, he even remains with any of his senses, while all his senses are with his beloved, still another moment: "Did I not love the smoothness of the 'R' it would perhaps not have come to 'by three rooms,'" but now enchanted away from the sweetness of her beautiful justification, richer than rich, as the lover could himself give himself, "but in the drunkenness," as the only lord, as incontestable guide of movement, "After all the swerve really becomes the word," room is no longer room but sound, valleyed, meaningful, full of sense, creation, "Lust becomes validity": lust creates that which is as it is: all of man thus does the whole, the unified. From lust of drunkenness, from the desire to grasp the drunkenness, "The very unique," but since I know that what is unique cannot be more so, and I nevertheless have used the twofold intensification as ornament and strengthening, and because I feel that here there is an unclarity and here people could come and point to it I feel a hatred for them which, however, is at once suspended in the security of my word: "The word which stands there against every reflection"; and now we have it, the completely unique, unsayable, the moment, drunkenness, happiness: here it presents itself, we can feel it, grasp it, here it is that the wholly unique becomes "readable." Full of happiness I thus sing, "reeling" in which I am blessed, but now, remembering that unclearness between logic and drunkenness, I want to hold on to it faster so that I see more clearly, formula-like expressed in the haste of drunkenness: "lovingest seeing," and back to the view through the window as if I looked out really "into the sea, above the sea," the magnificent, beloved looked-at one, "it clears wide under my window," is clear and clears itself and clears me, I call to myself who rests in happiness and again more easy, more confident, more promising to succeed, up to "reeling," for this is which alone is my friend, "with which I am alone," but it also is that by whose onrush I come most unified to myself, "with which alone I can be if I am myself." Come on even more strongly, I call out to it, "Call on me," tell me precisely the task, for I want to do it, how should it not come out of the deepest wine jugs, the drunkenness, now in the images too, it's coming "what in the years fermented in the sea and filled the drunkenness from which I was far away"—now I am living in the wine and lived in the sea, in the great salty flood, and if I now see it beautiful, it is because I no longer live in it but with the wine, for the pure hall is cold, and under the plain of waves are monsters. "Pour" now then, yes, everything already is wine, but the only glass, let it come so that I drink it and thus know for sure "I'm holding the glass," its bottom is far from the rim and darker than the clarity of the flood, "deep, and it presses against all clarity of the sea," surely it will conquer it, no, I am no longer wholly innocent but between sea and wine, it is not quite ordinary, the sea, the sea no longer counterpart, as if itself determined by the drunkenness, remembered the earth: "the clarity of the sea which begins at the mountain's spread"—the drunkenness is a miracle also for the sea, a wonder which sanctifies its own movements "and knows that the dark drink blesses the tides."

3

What do we have now? What has the foaming-out of the drunkenness offered us? What insights have we got out of it?

Perhaps because the author of the Beginning and of the piece we just left is the same, it was possible instead of making smaller to enlarge, instead of cutting into pieces to make clearer, perhaps because that drunkenness was that idea, now empathic seeing has served to make it splendid. The impression in the meantime is that of a more secure foundation, a more indubitable beginning.

To be sure, when we, as we did, following the course of that first piece, wanted to clarify it, we had to proceed in its spirit, the poetic one—in a different manner from that we'd have adopted had we done two different things which are possible: clarification of meaning and aesthetic critique, both of which, however, were not considered. On the first presently; the second we can touch on quite briefly and thus do so first.

Aesthetic critique, that is, the consideration of sound weighing and sound effect, thus the balance of them, hence of the relation between something vaguely in mind, thought, or image, idea or sound, color, form, lines, feeling, impression, coercion by light, and the expression, choice of words, placement of letters, the structure of syllables and sentences—all of this would be the task of literary-aesthetic investigation, thus is a separate matter which does not belong in the interpretation but is alien here.

As to the meaning, on the contrary, we can say already now that in the course of the following interpretations, that is, the consideration of the additional pieces of the first part this meaning will have to be increasingly paid attention to; more precisely, the significance of those additional pieces lies in their significance. If we juxtapose this statement with that other—everything is as it is—we see how already that first poetic beginning suggests a useful reflection. But if we first stop for a moment we observe ourselves how we, without hesitation and reflection, "suggested," say, thus harmlessly use an expression which would point to a wholly unclarified fact. How is this possible? Only because we surmise understanding and can presuppose it. Understanding by whom? For one thing, by ourselves when later we read again what was written, but then also by others—without wanting or being able to specify them. Yes, this at first unconscious but now conscious presupposition and certainty of understanding (or at least of the possibility of understanding) is presumably the guide of these lines, just as the guide of the first lines was the drunkenness. We called those lines poetic and these scientific—and thus we already have a hint at the two attitudes which, designated from the way the text goes, are both, "positions of being"

Thus on the one hand we speak of significance; on the other hand of being which is as it is, finally say that the significance of the additional pieces lies in their significance, whereas—so we must add—that of the first lies in the poetic. "Significance," however, presumably has two meanings. Significance means importance, for I want to say: the importance of the poetic and the importance of the significant; the first piece is important because of the poetic; the other pieces are important because of their significance; or the sense of the first lies in the poetic, that of the others in their significance. But here significance does not mean sense or importance, but what we can pick out from it, what we can lift out of it, what we can interpret, what we can infer. This situation thus is that the adequate sense of the first piece lies in its poetry, that of the additional pieces lies in the results of what can be lifted out of them.

Only now that we have gained a foothold for the distinction between the poetic and the scientific situation of being and have clarified "significance" can we with greater hope contrast the two statements, that everything is as it is, and the significance of those pieces lies in their significance. What does it mean to say that everything is as it is? This sentence surely is not abstract but relates to objects and more particularly to two quite specific ones: nature and spiritual, above all, poetic and philosophical utterances. When I say "the sea," "the tree," "the bird" are as they are, I want to say that no thinking, interpreting, poetic or scientific explaining exhausts them, exhaustively makes them understandable. If I know theories of currents, diffusion of fish, formation of coasts, melancholic, jubilating, anthropomorphic poetic works, philosophical conclusions by analogy of the sea of some kind, what do I have then? I have new aspects in which my own is mirrored, by which it is enriched, reflected in an interesting manner. What is my aspect of the sea? If I look out from the window (I am still in the same room), it waves; thoughts or images could come to me, as I am looking out, but my fundamental feeling when I see it, indeed when I merely think of it, is this: see the sea, there it is, there is the sea, it is. And if I were because of some particular circumstance about to give a picture of the sea or thoughts about the sea, I would surely take into consideration, in a more or less immediate look, what I have heard about the sea, but what would result, would be as it is, it would not be identical with a "description of the sea" or "feeling of the sea," it wouldn't let itself be expressed in fewer words than it contains. Just as little as the Trajan column is the same as a column with the details of the Trajan column, it is quite simply different, however much we have descriptions, photographs, impressions of it, and we, too, have only an impression of it. It is as it is, and we are as we are, and it is for us what it is for us—not its Kantian appearance. The more consciously its origin is made part of the intellectual utterance (as to a high degree in the present text), the more plausible it becomes that that statement applies not only to nature but also to intellectual utterances. If somebody asked me what I am working at, I would answer: Read it—not from impoliteness but because I don't know it any better, because I have no program, because I cannot express more briefly what goes on in myself, what comes out of myself: it is so because it must be so. I already said: in this writing, in which its writing is maximally made part, this is plausible. But it is true of all works, despite programmatic announcements. If somebody says in the preface that he intends to write on this or that in this or that way for such and such reasons for this or that purpose, this does not render what his book is. Others write or will write on the "same" topic: the essence, being the unconfusable of the book, whoever the author is, lies in that it is written word by word, comma by comma, thus and just thus: the book is the book.

But if everything is as it is, how is meaning possible? Surely, we answer, meaning, the various interpretations, belongs to the things, surely seas and books, locomotives and artists are by being what they are also are occasions of interpretation (and confusion). When we say, for instance, that a locomotive is a vehicle propelled by steam or electricity, running on rails, which serves to take people and merchandise from one place to another, have we by saying this said what a locomotive is? Surely not, for it also is a black moving something, or the expression of the time, or an achievement of technology, or a machine that diffuses soot and wind, or a thousand other things. What then is it? Is it one of these things? How then can it be the other? Or is it different things but not others? Or is it everything together? To this individual it is this, to that one that. To the engineer it perhaps is that vehicle of a particular kind, to the manufacturer of locomotives it is the result of production promising economic success, to the impressionist the moving black something. Thus, the locomotive is as it is but to every individual it is something else; it means something else for every individual.

Here is a brief insert that moves us on. Say that what was said is banal. Against this we hold that it is as it is: we shall see how it is when we see what it leads to. We shall return to this passage.

Meaning thus makes sense only in reference to two things: the object that means and the subject to whom it means. And the statement, everything is as it is, has its place only in a situation of being (or time) in which the human being cannot say, may it be as it may, for me it is this.

For the moment, applied to the present text, the drunkenness drives I don't know whereto, don't yet know its meaning, thus I can only say: this work is as it is, the creation brings forth the being, and only when it is can I take an attitude toward it, can it mean to me.

Let us consider another object with the same reflections. If I ask myself how I am, the answer is: I am as I am. If we bring concepts to bear—honest, mendacious, goodhearted, mean, intelligent, stupid, flexible—I wouldn't know how to say "yes" or "no" of any of them; I wouldn't know how to identify a single human being by such concepts. Every one means to me, and I myself mean to me, now this, now that. But doesn't something mean to me, isn't "honestly" something quite determined? Are words different here from things? Have the words changed so that they are ambiguous? Are they as they are, without any meaning? Have they got a thousand meanings? Are we living also with words in that time in which we can say only: they are as they are, and don't know their meanings? Hence I must create them anew? But I am just about to—now I can only add questions, only hold on to what comes to mind, without being able to think about it. But I don't believe that because of this tiredness something gets lost: the being created is so pregnant with meaning.

Questions: what tendency is this, what type of human being is there who says all this? Above all, who says that everything is as it is but has meaning—

what do the things mean? Can everything mean everything, where is the place of language? How is the translation of being into meaning possible? Can there be a connection between the sea and my thoughts about it? How does it come about that I am thinking all this? And nothing different or also only that a reader could think as missing here?

Let's then continue in the interpretation; now comes the second piece.

4

"Drunkenness," it begins, and I am again in a drunk mood. That I am in drunkenness, of this there can be no doubt, after the beginning, the event, the being of the writing itself had appeared so unbelievably after the years in the sea. Drunkenness thus exists, but I am afraid to be unable to know "where it aims at, what seizes itself in the drunk"—but the rock which appears when the sea sinks back? Is the sea the drunkenness and the earth what is firm under the feet, on what rocks are we being thrown? Earth also is the doubt, the question, not the unhesitating yes, the being in accord and consenting, but that which wants to hold us must know whom it is asking. And just those who only dip into the sea are precise: "Already the rock, but how much more crab- and snaildom ask what the drunkenness means, by what who is drunk and what is changed thereby"? Thus crab and snail do have the capacity for drunkenness, for they not only pose the question but already accept in advance the answer whatever it may be; they add: what has happened? Thus are as we are, or precisely we also have them in us, are crab and snail too, human being of an animal, sea, earth, and water. But a shudder overcomes us world swimmers already, we ask what has happened, but no longer earth question and crab question, sea and snail question, but moved into ourselves, pulled together into the tiny, icy vaporization above it: all of a sudden out of the living being the what-does-it mean, unimaginable detachment, which, however, is as the crab is, and this, of course, is precisely what makes us shudder; "The meaning." Back into the sea as a crab itself can get back anytime and disappears in the flood where it leads its life; I am lying on rock—preserved sea gargling, "But there I see from the rock, a square with movement carriers that changes uncannily": I cannot tear myself from what I see, on the contrary I am drawn into it having just now been pulled with a jolt into meaning and uncanny, anxiety-provoking, unlivable—into the other: if it were a crab I would know it but the square, which moves crabbling (just still walleyed aspect, "how desperate I would be if I could not hold it any longer even with these words, but this is threatening—are the words no longer clear?"—it is just still capable to thrust against me its being different, its nonclassifiability. But I notice right away that this large crab is different from me, that the impossibility of living oneself into it, however, is nothing bad, even that I can see it as it is, and it can be to me only by my watching it. And I, "I see the tender shell in the presoftened depth": I try to be like the shell or the crab but it is still more difficult to be shellman than crabman, for the crab moves but the shell rests; how is it, I am asking myself, I feel a comfortable pulling together to be glued to the rock, prepared, I mean, the spot where I am sucked fast, and since I am different I can mean only "in its heavy night," and yet see "how the green bulbous plants sway in the water wind," waving with the wave, billowing, already I am waving along, and what waves along is what I also was already and had: "the word 'theory' occurs to me but it doesn't come to mind, that's only more as earlier was or presented itself, it seemed to me, now, "precisely, I remember having heard it": I recollect myself, I pull myself, my different, manifold being, take myself together—transformations—and as the crab first infuses anxiety, so I now sense that word as Other, and since I am both no longer neither crab nor snail nor theory, I ask myself: "how does this go with the sense of a soft shell"—for this I have, this I am, too—"and fear of crabdom," for this after all I recently experienced too, this too after all I can be: in this condition I feel that this is different, of a different place, there is no hierarchy into which I could order theory and crab—even if each for itself were different but only one to me, for then I would be the order; no, "I can't say it more generally, no word or concept meets it, what crab means to me is unique," here the word crab just about still does as recently as the movement carrier was just about still valid, how waving the meanings have become and how much blind being urges forward, for me trembling one the meanings strike as helpless: it "is the crab feeling or the shell feeling," everything is still only as it is, if I feel cold and confused, "then so everything has a soul," and since this means that everything is as it is and since I know just this and nothing else, the consolation of this connectedness is only that someday I hope to see it more clearly, that one day everything means more than the meager being itself, only the heart is capable of such confused impressions, of such dark having, "named or not," for that small consolation we have that being is even if we don't always feel it, even if we never feel it: certain, beyond heart and name, it is that it is, even if this is only "heavy nightmare," and "the eyes close," nevertheless, just because we are having ourselves on this low ground, our being as being, being is certain for us. If until now this seemed poor to me, now I see the redemption in it. How could I in any way get to the mountain if it were not? But since it is, it can be no longer away from me through the split of unsayability, but I can now take it by the hand even though I climb up on it, and if (it is already like the shell in the presoftened depth) I crash down from it I am equipped with overrich jewelry, namely, crashed from the mountain. (Those who find this description rapturous or picture-like, don't see that here being and meaning are one: it is what it is to you.) Since a short while ago "theory" came to mind, it presumably is too, but since we are certain of being only now, it then was still "Thus there also is theory: what a difficult word, reachable only by means of equipment!": the hierarchy of being, which would give its real place also to theory, is missing, hence it is only quite unclear reflections of unknown origin with which we rinse this word, even spittle on it. Even if the reflection is as certain as this one: "To be sure, everything is theory," that is, as certain as the thought that everything is as it is so that the incontestability of meaning is missing, we nevertheless feel it as a pretext or yielding, explicitly to do away not yet with that which does not mean with certainty, the not-yet-meaning: "but who stepped back and gave it the name?" I do not answer for I am uncertain, but because I am a lover who is uncertain I have already found gold that does not dim even if it may change when I ask: "The idea of the last two paragraphs?" I must add right away: "What an idle, dangerous cover" (cloak of invisibility of weakness) "to call them theory! For everything is as it is, shell and word: a new sound," for the more it is the more it will show its being, perhaps even by going to be it will show this.

5
What did I just express? Thus, then, I may already ask. Accordingly, being permitted to say that by virtue of my writing down something that is written down, this being written down evokes in me a reflection on the basis of which I recognize that this being means something, so that I can, ever-more precisely reflecting on being and meaning, say something. Look as closely as possible: the first piece of the first part is what it is, that is, it is different from each of its meanings—as sea, poem, and everything—that is, is different for every being, for mine, depending on the situation of being, for your, for others? The being of the last sentence on the contrary—"the more it is the more it will show its being; perhaps even by coming to be it will show this"—is its meaning. For the last sentence means: the more this writing grows, the more manifest it will be what it is. We are thus no longer in the poetic, in which the human being does drunkenly, but in the scientific, in which he works with meanings. The poet, doing in the situation of being of drunkenness, creates being loaded with meaning; the scientist orders meanings. Soberly he orders the births of drunkenness, which attract him; his being chooses the meanings to order.

Questions: What is this being of the scientist that makes that choice? Is here the question of why appropriate, but not as far as the poet is concerned, for the poet's drunkenness is as it is, without why? Is there a why in the order of meanings, in the relation of being and meaning?

In the interpretation of the first part, too, we chose certain sentences, but differently: it was a following of the course of the piece. Here, however, it wasn't an accompaniment of being but an ordering of meanings, which came up with the meaning of our sentences because they appeared already in the sequence. Accordingly, there is an order of meanings.

6

"There still is giving birth." The work I am engaged in is full of the shudder that it may not succeed, full of coercion to remain with it, my confusion feeds on present remembrance, my hurry resembles that of the swimmer who, continually touching about in order not to hit the rocks, moves without thinking finally to reach the shore nevertheless. But he knows where it must go, I don't; still I believe that it is going toward something, rather more like a swimmer than one giving birth who does not know either, only the onlooker knows but is not it, only the woman is, but this being of hers does not appeal to her, she gives birth. If I leave my own being as it is and not how I could understand it through meanings, birth, knowing, doing would have no meaning which would be being, only being itself—but I also want to see ever more, but may I between the labor pangs rest a moment? Yes! "If I look out on the sea, the rock-sprayed sea, stones ringed by the sea, the sky, ship and man rope—tied now more tightly, now more loosely": it is not a mere looking—there as the woman in labor may occasionally notice the pillow or the wall, but seeing I am back drunk, at the rest moment of the birth which wants to bring forth meaning out of being, there is only the being that is seen. But how much I am comparing it with my situation of being, for I want to bring the law that created and directs my birth into the seen being by seeing what is lawful in it: the sea, the rock-sprayed one, it is in order with the sea-ringed stones, there is the sky, here man and ship, that is being pulled close: everything is as it is because it has to be so, there is no why, meaning is: "If I see on the little port square the girls seductively walking, the golden eyes playing green above the breasts and the hands around the laps"— as my being is ornated when I fall off the mountain, so is theirs by letting the golden eyes play green above the breasts and having their hands around the lap: the moment of rest creates being—"the baby already in their arms, the men dark trousers, laughing, already around the body": such is the order that I make up for what I cannot see yet, see what will be—and now already wholly the ornated being: "when I see the ice cream being sold, the cats playing on the walls," on which there also is a particular figure: "the old heavenly child, with lashed eyes, a fine nose and laughing mouth; when I see how the old man spits," and the richer the picture becomes: "how the ship is being equipped for the distant catch with the nets," the more it is the happiness of a dream (for necessarily we have accompanied already for some time the being, the interpretation has become necessary accompaniment of being which has meanwhile become necessary), "and now the wine covers, clouds, and suspends being in the strong blind image": out of the greatest jewel drunkenness and its image, wine, fall back together, the picture, when strongest, becomes blind: out of the meaning which is, out of the being of meaning becomes without why in the law of rest and birth being itself, and already again—the moment of rest is over—in the birth looking at child or coast, "light and sore in my heart," but this is how it must be: this light and sore is my being itself: "light because it is and I find myself face to face: there stands the word": being gladdens but now another being is at stake that must be given birth and since this is not yet and I, by letting myself fall back into the first drunkenness, find myself face to face with it, hence not yet I myself, it also pains: "sad and sore because I am not it"; but being all this, I feel light "because everything comes out of me," but "sore because my mourning hangs around it": the mourning which every birth has as being just like its joy.

7

Is it meaning which prevents me from considering or seeing the sea? Why am I writing these letters? I have to. Why letter by letter, finally the whole word, sentences, pages that are being numbered, a text of a certain length, why does this make sense? Because it's so. What cannot be asked? The being. What is the being? What can no longer be asked. Is the doubt? Yes. Is the sea? Yes. Is this text? Yes. What is not? What I doubt. Why do I doubt? Because I doubt. Do I doubt what for? Yes. Is then the what for? Yes. Is the why too? Yes. Where is no why? With the being. Also no what for? No. Where are why and what for? With the meaning. What is a meaning? That which for me is being. What am I? I. What is what can no longer be asked? Being. Am I being? Yes. Am I to me? Yes. Hence meaning? Yes. What am I doing right now? I am thinking. What is this? Going about with meanings. What am I going about with them for? To change being into meaning. When is being changed into meaning? When it is meaning. When then can I no longer ask of a meaning? When it is. Is thinking the meaning of my being? Yes. Is writing poetry the meaning of my being? Yes. Are thinking and writing poetry the same? No. Why? Because thinking is the transformation of being into meaning, but poetry is the creation of being. Am I therefore thinking, and making poetry in addition? No. But? Thinking I am, writing poetry I am, being I think, being I write poetry. Am I always? Yes. (Always?) Do I write poetry or think always? No. What am I when I don't think or write poetry? I am. What am I to me when I don't write poetry or think? Diverse things. What are writing poetry and thinking for my being, what meaning do they have for my being? Possibilities of my being. What is a possibility? What may be. Is the possibility? Yes: it is what may be. But are not writing poetry and thinking? Yes indeed. How then can they be? Because their being is possible. They thus are and may be? Yes: they are possible as being, they are as meaning. What is that which is as meaning but as being may be? Concepts. Thus being is being, meaning is what being is to me, concepts are what is as meaning what is possible as being? Yes. The glass is too, is to me, but only may be? Yes: the glass is, the glass is to me a welcome view, something out of which I can drink, I hurt against its ugly form, how small it is compared with the sea (similar to man)—all this is its meaning, its concept: the glass is not, here is no glass, or: here stands a glass—in every case it means to me this or that. Can I touch the glass? In certain circumstances: when it is reachable. Where may it also be? Elsewhere. What is this elsewhere? Space. What is the meaning of space for bodily things? Their place. Can I touch writing poetry or thinking? No. Thus they are not bodily? No, unbodily. What are bodily and unbodily in relation to being? Attributes. Are meaning and concept bodily or unbodily? Unbodily. Thus unbodily is everything, but bodily it only may be? Yes. Are thinking and writing poetry, which are as meaning, but as being can only be, bodily or unbodily when they are as being? Unbodily. And are they nevertheless not only meaning but also being? Yes. In order to know that the glass is bodily I touch it; how do I know that poetry is if it is not bodily but unbodily? Through the similarity of being. May possibilities of being also be elsewhere, do thinking and writing poetry, too, have their place? Yes: time. How do I call it when bodily things are in space, unbodily ones in time? They are real. Where did we start out from? From my being. Where have we come to? That my being can be real. But wasn't it real? Yes, it was, and it was just for this reason that we could arrive at its concept—only because it is temporal could we think of it as nonbeing. Thus, only because it is could we altogether think that it might not be. This thought thus is new being? Yes. Thus it is no thought? No. What thus is to us up to this point as the one thing that is real?

Why don't I proceed differently? Because I proceed this way. How does it come about that the order of the procedure looks as it does? I don't know; it must be my law. Do I know it, do I know its meaning? No, only its being.

How do I conduct myself face-to-face with this being? Trustingly, glad, strong. Thus I am changed, strengthened in my being by the being of the law? Yes; being speaks to being. Not to thinking? Only when that law wants it.

Why this paragraph in question form? Because it is so. Don't I yet know the meaning of this being? No.

Am I always? I don't know, but creating I am.

8

> Is rose in wine
> Is dawn in lap
> The sea!
> Black cone above the waters
> Always singing sound
> Oversound sings always
> if other it is yet the same
> above fishermen, fish and flood
> It pushes itself also over the threshold
> which I shall step on in a moment
> Is it the black darkness cone?
> Does it yield when I am inside?
> Does it make into dust or overcome me voracious of death anxiety?
> Sea of roses! Sea of death!

9

Something has happened, what has happened since yesterday? For in the meantime I have passed a night, again I woke up this morning, a bit also because of the flies, we are in July, I live in Camogli, this is how the place is called, and if it had a different name I would know nothing of this one, and perhaps it even is called differently, is merely called so, and I have no idea about the other, perhaps the more real one; still always in the same room, still always under me the sea, which perhaps is called being or altogether has not yet the name that for me is valid, but it calls on me as I am, and writing I am like the sea.

What has happened—I thought yesterday and in addition to what is on paper there was in me a crazy feeling, I saw the black cone that bent over my being, can I still stretch myself up, I asked myself, to breathe blissfully—yes, if I didn't perhaps know the air, would the cone not be terrible? Sea of roses, sea of death thus, but always sea, and since all content falls away, I am limited to pure being, poor salutary certainty.

What then am I seeking? Certainty. First find: the certainty that I am seeking certainty. What anxiety do I have in this search? I am anxious because I don't know the means and the landscapes in which I must seek. What thus far has been my means, which also unambiguously chose its landscape? To say only that against which I can make no objections. Can I explain to myself my crazy feeling of yesterday? Yes, for although I could make no objections to what has been said because it had been said out of necessity, but neither do I understand it. What does this mean? I don't agree with it. But what do I agree with? With all that is without my wanting to change it. But do I want to change anything whatever? No. Thus I agree with everything? Yes. Only not with what I wrote yesterday. I do, but I want to change it. How? By leaving it as it is but working on. How is it thus changed? It then is only one step. To where? Toward certainty. Am I not certain? Yes, I am. What am I seeking certainty on? On the necessity of the relation between that which I am and what is in me and that which it says here. How is it that I am uncertain about this? Because I don't know what the word is. How will I come to certainty about the word? By placing it because I have to. How is it that in this way I have certainty? Because that which I have made out of necessity is certain to me. But what I place out of necessity are words; they, however, will stand in certain relations and themselves be certain; but do I therefore know anything about the word? For instance, in this paragraph the choice of words has changed, I write among other things "place," which after the considerations thus far is wholly unknown to me, only "being" was certain to me as no longer questionable, but now I abandon that limitation because the questions are more pressing than the anxiousness in front of the unknown, but expressing myself in this manner I notice that today I am different, for yesterday I would not have spoken of anxiousness in front of the unknown; the law of yesterday, different from that of today, appears to me only as such, I label it thus, in reality, that is, when I consider this writing, a law that guides me was working, today it's a different one; what presses in me is accompanied by ever new being pressure and being tied together give birth in necessity—here is the most recent birth: only being, namely meaning-loaded word, can be born in this manner, but I seek certainty on the word itself: what is the word, I cry with words as man asks about himself; what I question only I can question only by means of itself, if there were no words and they did not have exact meanings for me, I could not be at all uncertain about them. Thus I know that the words have exact meanings. Meanings of what? Of being. What then am I afraid of when I know that the word is the exact meaning of being? That I might not be able to express myself. Was anxiety really anxiety? No, being that pressed for these words. Am I still afraid? No. Where did it come from yesterday? It is not quite clear to me—because I moved among concepts? Because I didn't try to express what pressed in me but stayed only among concepts; but since precisely this was my being that pressed for expression I felt like a jump over the unknown: being, pressure, concept are known to me as being, but the transition from the being that presses to the concept which after all is too, this makes me anxious. If I now try to look at it more calmly (if the anxiousness yesterday were not a consequence of being, today there would not be the calm that can look at the anxious-making being): I wanted to create the concept when it is already, that is, cannot be created; thus there remains only the task of producing the order between being and concept, better: to express it, for it, too, is. But aren't word and concept the same (for that which is to be expressed here)? Indeed so; thus the concept is precise meaning of being. Am I now calm? Exactly so, in order to be able to get at the interpretation of the fourth piece, hence to get at it. And happy? I have written two pages.

10

(". . . sore because my mourning hangs around it.") "And . . . I am still cringing with womb pain and uncertainty," I don't yet know what is being born, "and be it only about the image of the birth," for I am uncertain even whether the name "birth" renders unambiguously the being which I now am, and still, it is this birth "which must still be described": for even if doubt and anxiety and certainty of birth are already created in being, being transformed into words, there is still missing the name by which, if one thinks of things born, one recognizes just mine and holds on to it so as to be able to order it into the treasure of things which are, meanings and provided with names, "for where would the tree be if we didn't say: this is it," and also the spirit, the uncreated and creating being, wants a name in order to come into the order, its name is its bearer and what named things it has created: "and the spirit if we didn't say: he has it?" But by saying so, I name what presses to come out of me. If I say the tree is and this one has the spirit, then don't rely on the words, they mean more than themselves if you don't know that you yourself have set them down as valid, only if you know this do they mean themselves, are valid: they mean certainty about the being of the tree and certainty that he has the spirit, that is, not nothing, as it seems if you hear only themselves, for then they would say, I know nothing about the tree or about the spirit, and your certainty, seen from the words, would be deception and a treacherous attempt at ordering: "This somebody has called theory, but I feel and say: it is. "Thus certainty that I create being, and as this knowing and knowing again is being that is becoming, I do and know: "And as it becomes we have it increasingly." Again I rest, this time for happiness and certainty of birth, it is more a holding, drunk-like it starts, "For the wine is wonderful," drunkenness of happiness is overcoming me, this is why I know why the wine, something other than I am, is itself wonderful: if I am in luck, the other becomes good: the picture that I, seeing now, create, orders what it creates: "the rock is blueing under the green sea, the sea is blueing under the green of the coast's fall!" In a picture larger: "It is pale under the resounding tent and deep violet it shines up through the deep deep cup": for in the drunkenness I hold the wine against the sea and see through its red the order after which in the picture itself the darkness comes through the drunkenness. Thus, as drunkenness, being, and picture are only ordered picture, there is enrapturing unity: "An embrace are rock and sea under the white sun" and I with it "in the little room I sit with wine and pen in the finest noon above the sauntering sea." For even if the sea is as it is, saunters without my being able to follow it, and saunters even when I am elsewhere, it can be only because I am and because it is, namely, in my certainty is as it is being the sauntering sea. In this drunkenness "Flown away are Pan and the Fairies who never were": are they, too, figures of drunkenness, unfathomable clarity, but not I, neither my creator nor my creation were as now I am, they only were dispensers of enchantment, my drunkenness, in which enchantment becomes clarity, does not come from them, now I need nothing else but myself "because I already will no more do with sounds." But what happens now? Pan and the Fairies as flown are still in the picture, but the sound, not only sound but lure, the drunkenness poses the sound as new dispenser of drunkenness, and while the new drunkenness sounds I in the drunken sound go slowly out of the picture. What is this new drunkenness? "Already it flies before my eyes, beslavered, hostile friend, the ear"—the drunkenness is, was beautiful, whether the new one will be? Come, new drunkenness, you lure like a friend, don't take me away from the old miraculous drunkenness! Alas, but "I smell it, even in the fingers it slips already all in labor and as the new drunkenness comes on more significantly than I felt in its onrush and as I am wholly out of the picture, drunkenness and labor themselves, I am falling into a new picture: I am looking at the sea, which no longer is the sauntering one but is as I am and therefore we shoot together: "out of the fishing port shoots the fishing boat," but where is the womb: distant: "its mast is already at the horizon": now still pain of distance, but also picture of distance, and thus also close, namely making happy: "distant, near only to itself," I am losing myself into the picture: "the boat just goes along with it" and has voices, and "the crew neighs with salt and "bliss" of the new drunkenness, certainty of birth, I am quite ready, ever readier I am, there is always the equipment, the necessary one: "Wine jar and water jar, table on which it writes," and in the drunkenness of being ready and certain, the sea is more than itself and richer than only sauntering, and if I first only know that it is deep when I entrust myself to its depth and its sauntering: "deep the sea," and if I curse it because of its depth it is certainty that is also cursed, and when it is smooth I won't be the lesser for it, as I love it I become like it: "cursed, smooth, lovely one."

11

And now that I am in the drunkenness of happiness, the words are as they are, that is, what I am, and I am what the words are, incarnate, creation, and I am so certain of them that I can ask: "As if I hesitated!" But I don't hesitate, loving-beloved, happy one, who with playful tears wants even more: "Like a boat in ecstasy, but it is still not wavy enough to scream with dance and trilling death." The death dance since I live so strongly? The trilling of death? Don't break! I cry wholly deaf with love, "Death, come with your seed!" Image, destroy yourself! "Swallow flight, dizzy the air!" Bigger than life is death, more blessed is birth than love, I want to be birth giver, not happy lover, "Tears, choke the burden!," already I invoke misery that it destroy blind love, already it is the deadly drunkenness of life, the birth: "Break out, my arms, with lust!" everything appears weak, murder too, so close to death, and nourishment, so close to lust: "Lust, my laughter, bribe murder and nourishment!" Only the inexpressible is, the feeling, and if I killed lust and body, I would still the eternal breath: "Moment, fly up like a winged scythe, mow the world, my body its shell," no doubt that I would be extinguished with the world, "which drones and heaves," only this "world bloodbeat." And now, blessing image that blesses me: "When I rest, how it smiles to you, fruits to you, morning, my carpet."

12

Prefatory Remark
I hesitate to write and postpone it although I not only feel that I have to say something but even know some of what I have to say. Why then am I hesitating? Because just that which stands here may stand here but that which I have in mind may not yet? And why? Am I only writing what I have written and write "in full doing," but not or not yet otherwise? How is it that I feel that I may not yet write it? I can answer only: because here I am full doing but not with that one.

Well: what I am writing are words which I write because I have to. But is it here so that out of necessity occurs the act, out of the ineluctable (*Unumgänglich*) comes the processual (*Vorgänglich*)[1], the writing out of pressure like the child out of labor; is the issue birth which is because it must be? Or not?

No! For when I say I must write I have not yet said what I must write. What must I write? Accounting for what happens while, because I have to, I account to myself for what I am writing because it happens; there I achieve what I must, and out of the ineluctable of the writing becomes the processual of the meaning. Saying this I thus say that the processual is visible, capable of being considered, thought about, and usable for thinking—for otherwise it wouldn't be processual. But is it not just the same with the ineluctable? Is not also it, are not also the first pages of this text stimulating, can we not think also about them or perhaps let ourselves be drawn to dreams? Yes; and yet we have made the distinction, and yet it is right, for these lines really have a character different from those. What then is the difference between this processual and that ineluctable? Ineluctable is that which cannot be struggled out of; processual is what proceeds. Earlier I said out of that which is as it is becomes meaning, which is, but now I see more distinctly, correctly, clearly, unambiguously. In the beginning there was drunkenness, that which I could not struggle out of, and this in a double sense: first in the sense of unavoidable, but also in the sense that I cannot get around it. *Unumgänglich* has been translated as ineluctable because it was too wise and large, or because my strength was not big enough, or because I didn't even know where it was. But now out of this ineluctable has become the processual, that is, that which goes before our eyes, and here too in a double sense: first in the sense just mentioned, but also in another, temporal-spatial sense: it goes earlier or closer, before something else. Ineluctable, not being able to bestride, not passable, not describable, not to describe, not graspable, ineluctable happens; what is accessible to us happens only as processual; the ineluctable is ineluctable, other things go on, proceed, ineluctably goes forth from the ineluctable the processual.

The ineluctable speaks to us through words, which are its signs. The word is the processual means of the ineluctable; when we hear it, it goes before every other audible which therefore is temporally later, spatially farther; it goes before our eyes, ears, brain, heart, before all organs through which it is accessible to us—but the ineluctable is not accessible, not processual. The word "ineluctable" itself is nothing else but sign of what it designates, it is neither concept nor image, not thinkable and not imaginable. Do you feel what is happening?

The first pages of this writing, drunkenness, those words ineluctably come together, ask you the same, and so it comes that they ask you in their wholeness, and you are asking them only in their wholeness. They are the ineluctably processual means through which the ineluctable speaks to us (where, by now it goes without saying, the word "speaks" can only hint and wants only to hint) like that "do you feel." But what are the words themselves?

Theme: The Word

If I try hinting at how the first pages came about I say that I hastily and drunkenly wanted to exchange for words the press in myself, not in the sense of description or expression but of wording, so that the words are nothing else than the pressure itself, that is, the ineluctable as processual, and for this reason it is not single sentences, let alone words, which have validity, but only the whole, only the whole mediates the happening: the single, the word as word, separated from the happening, mediates only the incomprehensible, the false. What on the contrary is happening now? Now I am talking about the word, I am trying to learn more clearly what the word is, relating it to the distinction ineluctable-processual and to other experiences and reflections. To this purpose I use and need words, just as I had to have to render processual, to word the ineluctable, the pressing. But while I tried to point to my two activities, I also pointed to the fact that two different kinds of the use of words were at issue. The first I called wording, the second, words as expression of thought.

In wording, the word is both ineluctable and processual. Ineluctable because not to be struggled out of, processual because visible, accessible sign of the ineluctable itself. The becoming processual of the ineluctable is creation. But what have I created? The words, not the word—not the word in two senses: not only that as single word it is not new but also not as sign; only the whole—the words—is new, as grouping and as sign.

How now is the transition between those ineluctable-processual words to these which are expression of thought? I said I had to account for what happens, but what does this mean? It means that I confront the single word with the new whole of words, that in single words I want to express thoughts about the origin of which I know nothing. In considering what happens they have come to me, as if what happens, the ineluctable, had whirled them up. I understand why I know nothing about their origin: the ineluctable is not processual: what is at issue are more or less clear thoughts; I already see in the fact that I wrote "Prefatory Remark," then "Theme: The Word," that is, that I already want single words to have validity. But don't I quite simply want to understand the ineluctable? Indeed. But is this possible? No, and this is the reason why it's not single thoughts that are valid, why it isn't the single word which has validity, but here, too, only the whole, for here, too, the issue is wording, to be sure of a different form, but as soon as I want to go by the single word I am again drawn into the whole if I don't want to fall into insanity. Not long ago I didn't know this yet: then I wanted out and was drawn again into the ineluctable: sea of roses, sea of death.

Well, then, is the single word valid? No, but its validity is the task. What is the word?

Notes on later tasks: In a letter, whose recipient is better known than the recipients of all other kinds of writing, the single word comes closest to being valid, precisely because the single words relate to the ineluctability of the recipient, because in feeling with it he answers single questions (the letter itself is not ineluctable: wording in the second, still unclarified sense?). Two types of people: if the whole of words, not the single word is valid, then one cannot respond to the single word but only with one's attitude. For the other type the single word is valid, the single norm, the single law, the single statement, to which he or she responds by being this or that way, having these or those characteristics. Today the noblest is attitude; we no longer believe in the single: if I say "noblest" it is valid because I know ineluctably what it is to me. Is the ineluctable intentional? Not according to the word, for it is not accessible, how then could we declare something processual like intentionality about it? And yet thoughts, something processual, come out of it. Perhaps that which is valid as single has fled into this, our feeling for intention, into this processually questionable; the reason would be that today the ineluctable is felt only when it is felt as such, whereas in times when the single was valid, people were hit by deadly or divine confusion when they wanted to abandon the single. I, on the contrary, was threatened by it when I tried the reverse road.

Now the sixth piece of the Beginning, after the thoughts that came to us have come to be expressed.

13

"But now it is still noon": drunkenness, but not the first morning to which fruit is born, toward which I throw fruits which it gives to me, but light "and wine and sun are strong and weak in the air": wine and sun noon and at the same time themselves, intoxicating, not pushing, thus wine and sun, the strong and weak ones, again only noon in the air. "Will they let me?" I ask therefore for I no longer know whether the noon is not blind in them by lasting so. Have I, obliquely through the radiance, seen them too distinctly? Am I only depressed, and everything flees from me? "Does it seem so because I see them?" Is senseless seeing senselessness, death, insanity, staring? But I tear myself out for I am asking, now already observing what's happening: "Has the drunkenness gone?" and as if nothing else could follow, I add in great confidence: "Is the birth going on?" And actually, away from the other, away from time of day and landscape, toward the birth, toward doing, to writing: already there is memory of what was done and of drunken past, already they are strong enough to stand and to radiate, wonderful thoughts detach themselves from the cliff as do law-like water eddies moving back from it when the ineluctable woos the processual: "Certainly, I am no longer so choosy with voices and colors": the processual already entrusts itself to the happening because love sinks in more willing, for the rock, too, woos the sea: "it's closer," for it only seems to have been innocence, modesty, childishness, which ask me to call it "it" instead of "the ineluctable": this could not bring us closer, and only through its transformation into itself it becomes the new word structure that makes me happy: "Thus, no what," for the whole that just now appeared was the answer, and "no loss because drunkenness would appear less drunk": it did transform itself into itself, now is so to me while earlier it was drunkenness, thus "only: so it has gone," remember, and addressing those who happily feel along with the becoming of the processual my happiness and certainty appear in a new mirror: I invoke already among them the remembrance of the time of drunkenness when I jubilated: "give me the hands full, the law": what was invoked is here, is the law, wonderful fulfillment.

In words which no longer are the wording of the ineluctably processual but which mean themselves, that is, which are expressions of thoughts and only for this reason mean themselves, thus are thoughts about the origin of which we know nothing, which we only feel; otherwise said, we can (must!) accordingly express ourselves: is what is at issue here the turn which we cannot word and express in thought other than thus: from the ineluctable to the processual—said, accompanying being, interpreting, it was in the happening: "This then are the first blows with the cold chisel: no matter how often I go over it, the sentence stands, clarified by the observation that this is the course of this writing." From the ineluctable to the processual; being, it said (not yet I, for "I" presumably corresponds to saying, only the I says—in front of the ineluctable, it, happening) is that which cannot be questioned, in this sense there is talk about the sentences: now it says: it was the ineluctable, it is the processual. And quite processually it continues (processually but *it*), and even if in images: images are characteristics of words, not kinds of words (like wording and thought expression): "When we later enter more sober fields in which there is digging going on; when we—to imagine the landscape already—speak more abstractly, imagelessly": this means the consideration of what happened and sees that it availed itself of other kinds of words which mean themselves, as we now know, but why abstract and imageless, without knowing what "abstract" is, it merely wants to suggest that the issue here is not drunkenness, and that "imageless" still confuses characteristics with kinds of words: here the words are ineluctably processual, but valid only in their whole, while earlier they were already valid as single words but necessarily pointed to the whole, that is, were thoughts; and yet, what we have is by no means a relapse, for the single is not taken as valid. And because there is still drunkenness, it continues: "or—to name it from the present," when we "are simply different," consider the single: when does the form of question in which the whole sentence stands and which expresses in in-case-of and the later time—if it occurs we know at least what is to be done, but we are still too much in the drunkenness to be able to know whether the processual proceeds, comes forth; neither do we know that we don't know anything about the origin of the thoughts, and thus the trembling question: "is there a transition?": here the whole sentence lifts itself up, and by talking about it now have only taken out of it what is in it, thus for the first time in the interpretation have actually interpreted; there suddenly the whole is no longer valid but the single, and interpretation suddenly means itself, the last question means itself. But since I now really "pressed forward, that is, that I must speak of the ever greater nearness of the validity of the single, these sentences mean ever more single things, namely, themselves, and we thus are already deep into the processual without being able to ask whether perhaps still something of the ineluctable could be contained: the uncertain origin of the thoughts confirmed itself and with it the reality of the ineluctable and the processual, and their transition or jump or going forth one out of the other cannot be identified other than as ineluctably processual: since it is ineluctable it can only be felt ineluctably processually (as we can only hint at).

If I read how it goes on after the last interpreted sentence, it strikes me as a dream, and it may well be that the "transition" referred to, about which we know nothing, is a dream, where the dream would be related to it like the ineluctable to that which is ineluctable, and we could call the dream like the ineluctable a sign. "Does the road lead not from Dionysus to Apollo"; for here I place two deities, of whom I have only a weak notion, at the place of the ineluctable and the processual; in the case of Dionysus I do two wrong things: he himself means only himself as now the ineluctable means only itself; but as I (as a non-Greek) posit him he is only a mask for what happened to me: this, however, I did not yet know, and thus it is that I believed that I could posit images, make the single valid, while here only the whole is valid: dream piece. I made the same two mistakes with regard to Apollo: he, too, is only a mask and not for that which he was, namely, himself, but image of the god of science, image of science itself—but Dionysus and Apollo are understandable and valid only in the whole while that for which they are images which in the pressure came out wrongly, they are valid, ineluctable and processual, as singles because they mean themselves—to be sure, they, too, show their ineluctability only in the whole of this writing—and thus is confirmed, even though as something not yet overcome, the distinction between wording and the expression of thought.

But actually, it doesn't go back to Apollo "but to the microscope, and how?": here we have a double approach to the validity of the single: first it is noticed that Apollo is still too much himself— at that time when writing this one would have thought that he was still too godlike—that with him what was in my mind could be caught (so we say now; in reality, however, what was in mind was not the processual, but Apollo was to have represented science): thus out of the whole and toward the single, the intended; and on the other hand, the microscope really is the image of what is intended, namely, the processual: the single that is before one's eyes when the eyes look through a lens; the microscope, excluding what else could be in eyes and senses; it is the most palpable image of what is meant. And thus the question is cleared: how it is possible that the drunk, the inexpressible, and incapable of speaking all of a sudden sees only the single. How does single become out of the ineluctable and its observer? "Surely, Dionysus avails himself also of the microscope," this is not the issue, we too have availed ourselves of words in drunkenness—but just then it is after all not the words but the wording, just then it would not be the microscope but the drunkenly grasped with which the doing is drunk—and if we imagine it, the microscope is valid only in the whole of this image (new confirmation of the dream thought: it, of course, is understandable that also: "Dionysus does avail himself of the microscope"); has validity of the whole, thus is ineluctably processual; but now appears in the interpretation: as, of course—ineluctable-processual synthesis—dream, dream): the question rather is: "but how does he get there? Does he step out of the drunkenness, why is he no longer drunk with himself, what transition is this, what changes because of it, "and does he remain the same?" And the question already posed here finding only an image expresses a single thought, which, however, comes somehow—again it is being confirmed—out of the ineluctable.

This thought stimulates another: "Up to now we can know only: what is here is for our condition the road, and for that later one it belongs to its knowledge": expression of the fact that the dreamlikeness of the text must be felt and an accounting of its meaning be given; at this moment the points of relation are still lacking, is still lacking the place where could be put what is in it; what is missing is accompaniment of being, and for this reason it is recognized only as wording, as processual-ineluctable; yet the single is already valid so far, there is thinking already of such kind that the later state reached in the dream, the consideration or interpretation is likewise recognized as processual-ineluctable and what is more: provided with the quality of looking back, which is addressed to the dream. "How the question lures!" But this is no longer a thought, this again is wording, even if Dionysus, who avails himself of the microscope, the drunk one who sees; neither image nor thought, neither image of a thought nor image in the wording, a dark sentence, as if whipped up to the aim, as if the ineluctable intended the thought, like a sign of its intention, a veiled pressure—nothing but images in order to feel the unknown.

14

I thought, thoughts about the ineluctable and the processual, what they actually were, would be necessary (and these thoughts would then of course have followed), but while I also was in doubt about this expectation, I accidentally found the second volume of Musil's *Mann ohne Eigenschaften* (*Man without Attributes*), leafed through it, I don't know why. Suddenly the idea came to me by noticing (not yet at the first reading some time back) how much his book amounts to the presentation of "today's" human being (even though countertypes are not missing, of course, and the expression, the image, comes precisely out of the whole) that I myself said that earlier one had had qualities (and today attitudes or positions); fugitive thoughts followed, in the form of expression, his the novel, mine different (not here to think about the possibility of its designation or its designation itself); proud, I thought, he ought to be of so much work, but at the same time: how can one choose such a title? For me this would be unthinkable; my own works don't appear to me such as could have a title: if I don't know anything more than that the inexpressible urges me to express things, these things are far too intimately connected with the urge for it to be possible to lift them off giving them titles! But can the title, I objected to myself, not itself be an urge and not a reflection (which, that is, would be false)? Yes, this could be so (I had to admit, from experience), but here this is not the issue. For Musil's urge is not toward blind doing, but to present his thoughts about the time, his experiences with the psychology of the type of human being he observed and thought up, and this in the form of a novel, creating situations in which more clearly than by means of observation, appears before his own eyes as well as ours what he wants to say. An antiquated manner, a still processual manner, too much gathering (contemplation and collection) for it to be enough. But I doubted whether I should say this, looked out of the window, sat down on a high antique chair, reflecting on what could be the result of it (of insights), apparent to myself (look! I called to myself) like one who speaks from the chair of a judge or an orator to others, at once a greater attitude, at once more significant content, at once more important, more confidence deserving sound, whistling, back again on foot in the room, around the furniture, false by intention, into interesting neighbor's and enemy's, a familiar (banal, dear) popular song, thought, thinking of the sounds, to where do you scramble through, swerving, it came, I was even more certain, was therefore reminded of a sentence by Hofmannsthal, "In the deepest enchantment that you have undergone" "your self is to be found," how can, it whispered all the time in the midst of it, the single (processual?) mean—but it did have meaning without Musil's book, thus for me (?) on the other hand (thousands of hands) have others, have not also Musil and Hofmannsthal done their deepest or best by their ineluctable manifested in the single, and why is it still not enough for me? Because I am different, certainly, because we (who?) are different, probably, I always want to throw myself into the poetic, a novel, I called to myself, write that, so the eternal interpretation would fall off and you could do what you wanted and not what you must, but then there too, is Must and here too, is Wanting, thus how is it? Swerving I became certain, the sentence stood however often I examine it, it remains in existence, here, I thought, we perhaps have a way for finding out something more exactly about the ineluctable and the processual: the sentence lives only in the context; one may, one must accept it without understanding it, but yet not differently from my now having to ask what the sentence means: since what is certain is what stands here thus far, so is this a sentence too, not the words since the words in it are the only thing I can hold on to, coming from elsewhere, considered with respect to their relation, will receive new meaning, perhaps validity   validity!

Go then, and already the sentence demonstrates itself also so that one can feel with it: swerving I am getting certain of myself, what does swerving mean, what does certain mean? But just this must now be explored; out of the swerving rises the single, that which can be considered.

Swerving already presupposes the I, thus we must ask first what the I is. Already with this thought we have gained something, namely, the following reflection: doesn't it seem as if the predicate "green" remains itself, no matter whether I apply it to the sea, to a leaf, to a bottle—the predicate "swerving" by contrast not? Let's try to express the situation in relation to processual and ineluctable. A statement like "The sea is green" has been called a synthetic judgment because I form through the composition of two acquaintances, "sea" and "green," a new one, "the green sea." In this activity, objects and means are processual: in my head go on: sea (above all else) and green (above all else): the objects and the means of their connection: the positing as a quality. The Kantian question exists no more. Whereas he, in order to explain how this synthesis should be possible, answered with the structure of man which, he claims, is such as to say to the ineluctable "sea" and to the ineluctable "green" and to the ineluctable "The sea is green," we cannot, precisely because we see how ineluctable all this is (sea, green, and statement), be satisfied with the way of becoming processual. In the first place, we recognize rather only that the statement is valid as a whole, as wording, precisely not as declaration, precisely not as synthetic judgment. But is Kant's view therefore wrong? No: to see how he saw was for him ineluctable. But did he perceive the ineluctable as such? No (but transcendence with its formal and continual consequences). What excites us is the task of translating the ineluctable into concepts, into the processual, for it is no concept, it is, also logically, only what it is. We can no longer ask how synthetic judgments are possible because we know that which for Kant was a synthetic judgment isn't for us since synthesis (and analysis too) takes place in the processual while for us it appears as follows: I behave ineluctably toward the ineluctable, as I notice only by the fact that the sentence "The sea is green" proceeds for me. Process thus is neither "green" nor subject-predicate but only the whole, and when I say that I have no means whatever of letting the single proceed for me, I am saying the same thing, for if I had such means, the whole would be the synthesis of what is known to me and not processual as a whole.

Now I understand better (and so I hope one understands better) why I said that the single is no longer (or not yet) valid, but only the whole. We now also have a clearer view of the ineluctable: it is that which I do ineluctably, how I do it, namely, ineluctably, and the result of my doing too is ineluctable and therefore effective as a whole, but processual by virtue of the fact that it is effective at all. I cannot come closer to the ineluctable in any manner for otherwise it would not be ineluctable; but everything created out of it is in relation with it: it mirrors it, it is its image, it confirms it in many diverse ways, all I say, feel, think about it is merely my way of experiencing it: there is not yet its incarnation, unless it be this writing: certainly imperfect, but as certainly ineluctably processual.

Swerving I get certain of myself: the single, what can be considered, which rose was not the I, the wavering, the certainty, but what just preceded, ineluctably preceded, thus was not the simply processual but again only the whole. Thus in the ordinary understanding that sentence makes no sense, and this feeling of senselessness is the despair of those who do not see its new sense, they are still attached to the processual, to logic, but would have only to consider the word *Anfang*, beginning, to see it speaks only of *Fangen* (catch) and not of the area and the means of the catch; on the contrary, thinking is never *Anfang* but movement in what already is going on. In thinking now I am certain that I have already caught the processual. In swerving, I am getting certain: from the whole to the ineluctable, from there to the processual.

15
(In blind jumps I am running gigantically over the earth, snakes collect already under my feet in my shoes, stoolstones already trill toward me, already the sea bellows away toward other stars, whither? My eye burns, whither? My ear thunders, whither? My belly rages, whither? asks my whole being, waken from the deepest sleep, surprised I find myself high above everything created, with snake dung and water under the arm toward myself—happy one!)

16
If I say that even scientific books, biology, chemistry, anatomy are valid only as a whole, the opinion that I am an aesthete or represent an aesthetic picture of the world is fundamentally wrong. For to represent aesthetics or ethics or l'art pour l'art or any orientation whatever is processual doing: ineluctably it is not possible, for if aesthetics becomes ineluctably this can happen only in two ways: either the ineluctable is felt as such and from it the processual comes forth, but then this aesthetics is not valid as such, as something processual, but only ineluctable-processual, the mirror, we may perhaps say, of the ineluctable, a way of feeling it. Or the ineluctable is not felt as such but ineluctably the aesthetic is erected and in this process the matter is the same; we perceive today all aesthetics which remain not only the processual, which are only word orders, as ineluctable-processual, and just because I know to move on ineluctably I can be no aesthete: if I were I would not have experienced the fall into the ineluctable because I would not have needed to experience it: but then no norm is valid, there are infinitely many ways of experiencing the ineluctable, and the way of perceiving it as such is only one, is the one which today is processual; when the nullity of norms hits us, only the ineluctable is ineluctable; at one time an ineluctable expression was: the spirit bloweth where it listeth; today on the contrary it reads: the ineluctable is the one thing but in infinitely many ways the processual comes from it. But both sentences are as little wrong as Kant's synthetic judgment or his Transcendence; and by saying that they are only ineluctable-processual I confirm my one way of becoming processual: that only the whole is valid and the whole goes even more forth before: the way how out of the ineluctable the processual comes forth.

Conscious of the harvest which will follow, we interpret the last section of the first part, of the beginning.

Question: where do lyricism, science, philosophy, wording, expression of thought fit in here?

17

"What then—letting yourself glide into the sea, fructified, sea-benumber—is knowing?" In a double image is welcomed here the longingly reached process but also conjured processualy in the question there shimmers its possible unbelievability, the insertion reminds us of the time spent in the sea, certainly a throwing yourself into it which makes us happy, but also the knowledge is known to us only as something unknown, a half blind approval of what has been after all in drunkenness, fructified, sea-benumber, fructifying sea-conqueror—but, so the abyss is called, how can I and what can I do with the sea? But already here we perceive what leads the whole section to its valid pregnant end: that the processual for which the question stands as image, is reached in the drunkenness that is right away recognized as unknown, hence in an uncertain transition but nevertheless real, really reached and just to be entered. The reason is, we now know, that it was reached ineluctably-processually, as it cannot be reached in any other way. And thus we continue: "The question, the question pregnant with answer, ornated with answer: it is the drunkenness which holds something else": we feel for the first time a single question that goes ahead of all others and therefore requires an answer; thus no wording but loosened single thought which has its particular portentous look. Therefore the answer too must not be understood in the context but it is given in memory (process) of the drunkenness, of the wording, and by looking at the present contemporary, new, astonishing words; but just through this the answer to the question of what knowing is oriented toward that knowing that we have been communicated from the course of what has happened thus far: of it we know only what we can say about it, by no means what it is but only for us ignorant ones that are determined by what happens: the drunkenness which holds some other which for us now is called ineluctable, out of which something processual must come forth. No, but by relating what has happened to the processual, the processual question what knowing is was answered through the processual designation of what had happened; but since this is no answer in case the question appears processual, single, the whole play is valid only in the context, as a whole. And as we already then felt this unclearly, there follow many images of our condition: "the eye which shelters the other": I still feel only my convulsively watching eye and see nothing else than that it already sees other things; I already notice that the single swings along in so far as at least my condition comes forth and I am trying to express feeling this, I find the courage to call out: "the itch for the sake of scratching": hurt me more! I feel, for the deeper the hurt the more certainty of healing, I have confidence, it is ever more certain to me that the processual has been reached or at least is reachable. So great is the feeling that I call out to myself: hold on to it! Draw this point of the road: "(I walk about scratching my flea bites, the fleas come from a dog who no longer is here)" and everything on which the mighty drunk look falls is being sucked into it, the drunkenness gives it validity in the whole, the drunkenness of power gives it life—as the drunkenness of happiness made the wine good while misery was powerless and could not make the birth bad, and as the lover lifted the goosepimples into the love—and this too, mighty as I am in my confidence, I sense in my mind: "shudders of sickness and death as drunkenness: that which I, as a little one, knew as bad and danger is none, for I am great, as a little one I can say nothing, only in power, only now do I know what sickness and death are, "technique as life-heightening," even "brain as stimulant": everything operative, eluctable, being active ennobles and strengthens me, for I am mighty, even the statements which are possible only now only heighten my power, and as it is ever more confirmed how really the processual is reached, the more is valid what was answered in response to the question about knowing; I see that this is my processual, beyond logic, only what came forth, I also know this: the single is valid: "knowledge explains only at this stage," only in the here and now do I know it. But with this I have a here and now, now I can ask, now the processual has proceeded, is certainty and point of departure. "But drunk with ineluctability of being, this being, lifted up above the landscape from which the explanation grew, as being One like the pine (compared with the other as compared with the birch)": ineluctable birth, ineluctably born and ineluctably become as it has become. Thus pine, the pine law, my law: "Accordingly since no longer valid only for the landscape, is the logos, our inner structure which here ecstacy moves everywhere?" In the drunkenness of power I have stated, in the confidence of the processual reached, that it has ineluctably come forth; it appears to me as human to perceive now what happened as processual, image of the ineluctable, like pine, like birch, like power. So dumb, so wise, I ask: "Where does the tie to the landscape end, where does the new sound begin?" I know that birth is taking place here now, that is valid for the landscape: if, precisely, not everywhere: "How is it that something not only is as it is but interpretable or even unambiguous?": because it is so, I know, but I am looking for an image for the ineluctable, give me an image after the unending imageless time, I whimper and triumph; whimper because I know I myself cannot make an image, triumph because I know that I can do everything that is drunk in me and that in drunkenness becomes what in imageless time only still seems image, processual mask of the ineluctable; only I, I myself powerful birth, am in the time of images, "My child! My child!" I break out in the drunkenness of bliss and add in the drunkenness of the already wise one: "Let yourself be looked at, show yourself!" for it makes me drunk with new ineluctable coming forth.

Dreamward

1

Today I have a green pajama on as my day dress, green the color of hope, I was told. As my hand was touching my back as in a dream I didn't know whether I was touching the cloth or the skin. In the down of my belly I saw a white hair although I'm young. But even if the prophet is there, there are no people for him to preach to.

So that we may get acquainted I'll tell a story. I was planlessly walking along the sea on a road over a rocky green in the sun, saw a steep path winding upward in a fertile-looking, abounding, tree-shrubby, rough-sunny defile toward an unenvisigeable goal, self-sufficient and inviting me. I had hardly noticed it when I also felt a tremor in myself for me to enter it: not only in my blood so many green stumps, parts of snakes which were winding themselves, rearing up again and again, they were stumping up, making me uneasy, urging me on, away from the planless walk, pushing me, making me attentive to sea, road, the meadowy-sunny sun, until finally I found myself on the path already. The stump tremor increased, I went upward, I felt the pleasant sweat run on my forehead and along my body, it moistened my eyes, it pushed my face, it pushed toward the height. Even as I was stopping at almost every step it was less walking than a stop moving on, less climbing than becoming glum, less a stepping out than a dreamy amber. I saw fig trees' riches, the fullness of bushes, overpowering green, warmth, shimmer, being sucked into stone heat, hot, yellow, dry sand, little abysses everywhere, shaded by giant leaves, without sea, only for earth and world; benumbed depth, cursed brightly blue, stirring blue, stirring depth, it was a leaden, jewelled, ill-feeling curing walk. Really there, there I saw the first snake. This fright, in spite of all memories and all knowledge, in spite of sea and landlessness, of feeling sick, the blood-stumps, tremor, creeping in skin and cloth older than old in the young down, green in red—only red-green now. It swished across the road hardly seen, forefelt as an army vanguard, as a sign—this was the greatest fright, it could not be increased when I saw thousands of them circling toward me, beating against me, tremble, stump, rear, snake power. If I grasped for a tree it toughened, dripping with distinct secret and open death, my foot-over-snake cramped, I drew myself inward, if I only were a ball rolling over the world, where it falls it's its law, where it tumbles into nothing it is its ball sense. But still I was no snake yet, the snakes were still different from me, snakiness wherever I saw and heard, felt, dreaded, grasped, bent in despair, and only for the moment I longed to be torn high into the sky, into the snakeless blue. But only a moment, as I immediately remembered, for I knew that in the sky too there were none but snakes, that even the sky itself was a snake. Snake fly! Snake world—and now I saw the giant variety, kinds and singles, with snake fingers twisting on the snake forehead—"become yourself a snake!" I was shouted at with a double hissing tongue, and I knew myself a snake self, earth-creeping, sun-icy, I rolled myself about, monster—leave me this remnant—unendingly blind, lame, and deaf with nausea, but creeping snake mightily with my uniquely caught up drawn-in scale suck to and fro in myself, sea snake among sea snakes in the sea, earth snake among earth snakes on land, darkness snake under the sun—in the somber scales-sky—in my sudden infinite fall I, the mad one, noticed that a story was going on, old man in the growth of youth, my hope-dream skin, cursed, pregnant prophet to whom the peoples have died away.

2

It will still be quite different and much worse, you will live on cliffs and on boulders, needle-pointed, so that your feet would hurt if you could walk, but you cannot walk because your happiness consists of a rock fissure hardly to stand on, but the rock splinter penetrates you constantly; when it crackles in the air it is death all the time, and when the sea moves it is only practicing devouring you, it only is trying to overcome the nausea of touching you.

I dreamed a big fish, caught by thousands of fishermen, and a few of them had been slain by his movement—now they were stretching and expanding him, the giant ray, boasting, so that he darkened the glaring noon, and those who had stood in the sun stood in the fish's shadow, larger and larger they pulled him apart, he and the houses among which he stretched out so far were darkening the sky; there some suddenly shivered with the bigness of the fish caught. The friends among whom I was standing talked about how gigantic the animal was, but I, I urged them or us to go on and said: "There are much bigger sea beasts, and with them there is a peculiar story." There we came to a fish shop invited by something in the window that reminded us of fish—we hurried to get there, and although I was running I couldn't help smiling silently; and from the triangular fin, hardly visible far back in the store, they knew it was a shark, but one half of his head alone had already busted the window panes, and far and wide the people had run away and were no longer to be seen, were no longer in the air. Bristly, reddish, of a vehement form, it lay there, overgrown, bald, shiny, blunt, smooth and grainy, boulderlike, iron-hard, shark. "Now, my friends," I told them "this one is bigger than the fish they caught, and yet he too was caught, but the people have fled in terror before their booty. On this shark you'll have to live," my mouth was saying while my heart was being torn as the giant ray had been, "glad for the scale which will be your house, your hold a tiny pointed growth, beloved thorn and the near hasty red joy and dizziness of your eyes; without food, without work you last out until the giant, through a shake, throws you before his throat—when you move it is destruction, and only through your death will you feed the fish who now can be caught no longer. But "I," I said behind my friends who were staring sharkward, and I stretched, "I have my snake law." As they were snaking from their sites and turned round I heard their high shrill screaming, for I already was snaking myself toward the ray and shark sea to live in it, winding myself, wonder-swelled.

Snake Arms

Only the feelings I have toward these dreams: that they are of one cast and out of me, firm, unswervable, deeply, blissfully, and enrapturingly akin, and finishing, feelings as in dreams, feverish, I made them already by writing, they make me simple. I am quiet, a state has been reached, a transformation: the dreams, my creatures, I their creator, have thus become my creator, I their creature, there has been talk—a situation of which I well know that it is reached through transformation and follows other situations, it probably won't last until the end of my life, but I am no longer rushed, the ineluctable is no longer a hunted animal after which I, already bleeding out of all pores, scratched by thorns, wounded by stones, washed by tears, roared at by fire, stung by the deepest repugnance never to reach it—no, it is no longer so, I am myself the hunted animal, and however I express myself it is in myself, my arch home and refuge, my eternal support which, ineluctably akin, holds upright the walk itself. The world through which I am going, the world of mountains, is no less steep, of ghostly canyons, smooth like an elf, sun-hot, pointed, but I manage to walk for the first time altogether, I care no longer whether it is my world which I, wandering, make mine; because I walk them, the roads are new and I couldn't walk at all if the ineluctable were not in me, my five senses. I now know that there are roads; to find them is the task; there are outlooks and there also is love. What can it concern me now whether one day perhaps the ineluctable will be cut out of me, why should this not be simply a new situation, think of the transformation, it calls to me, and I think of the ineluctable transformation.

How was this transformation? I have seen it, have described, worded it, we know it, and now I know that the ineluctable has pushed me, and despite my blindness and stubbornness there has come forth what had to: I renewed, transformed, certain. If I think back to the harvest I wanted to have I had in mind to express in only one language what had grown in many plants, to order the various rock points so that they would be surveyable, as if they were alike. If I think back to the time shortly before the beginning I did not know what pushed me to writing, I thought the consideration of time and word, also clearing myself of course of life, Nietzsche, Broch, Musil, Joyce, sociology of knowledge, and the phallic primordial shudder. This all is there, I think, as fountain or road edge and rootstock, uncertain still how the roads go but certain of them and sure that I can walk them.

But how beautiful is now the landscape toward which I have dreamed, in which I have arrived dreaming, in myself. Therefore let me stay, my pressure, and rest and love, there I already see how you laugh to me and permit. Be sure, for I am sure: where you push me there I feel pushed, there I will go.

1
With the cloth of shame I covered my face and moved on.

Note

1. I translate *unumgänglich* ("un-goable-about," unavoidable) as ineluctable (non-fightable-out-of) and *vorgänglich* (an adjective of *Vorgang*, process) as processual. In this relation, the ineluctable is not only unavoidable, but unknowable, unnameable, and all claims to knowledge of it and to the capacity to name it are vainglorious or, in religious terms, idolatrous. And yet, as I am discovering this moment (much later), this text is an effort to approach the ineluctable.

CHAPTER 3

Hannah Arendt and Hermann Broch

Hannah Arendt's Letter on Vorgang

Now, before everything else, what Hannah Arendt wrote about *Vorgang*. I'll try to translate it from German into English, confident that this activity of translation will change the meaning of what she wrote.

8 April 1957
Dear Mr. Wolff-[1]

Vorgang has interested me uncommonly.

The snag in the matter is that the interpretation [*Auslegung*] in principle is infinite and that this infinity-in-principle, if it cannot in turn be contained [*gebannt*] in a poetic or cognitive [*denkerische*] form, dissolves [*zerfliesst*]. Already some things in the "Anfang" [*Beginning*] are Auslegung [interpretation; literally "laying-apart"] which again and again gets in your way. I don't mean by this the reflection which looks at the *Vorgang* as something *Vorgelegtes* [laid before, existing, being there] and then interprets [*auslegt*] it. It is hard to understand why you don't let the interpretation be followed by the interpretation of the interpretation. And if you think about it, it is even harder to understand why you don't keep on writing at this piece, the *Vorgang*, until the end of your life.

But I could very well imagine somebody who on the basis of a *Vorgang* [i.e., an experience such as I had had] doesn't bother with the continuation of life

[*Weiter des Lebens*] and instead, precisely, simply would interpret into English. In other words, the *Vorgang* [the event, the experience] would have so to be brought-into-one that the interpretation is written like a *Vorgang* [as an experience, as an event]. Of course, I don't mean by this that you should or could change this. On the contrary, only because you first made it the way you did could you perhaps also do it differently some other time.

Cordially greeting,
Hannah Arendt

First, there is the problem of translation. At a first glance, translation may seem the road to a solution in the sense of clarification. For it loosens the text, punching holes into it until—and here the delight of clarification waves ominously—the text turns foamy, into foam, the language which made it up *zerfliesst* dissolves, to borrow a term Hannah Arendt uses to name the threat of unending because unendable interpretation; but the threat of the text turning foamy is incomparably deeper: it concerns language itself. Language itself is not endangered by interpretation nor by unendability; it does not become problematic unless in one of the interpretations language itself should turn into its own problem.

The prime case of what is at issue here is the word *Vorgang*. *Vorgang* may serve as a road to the unfathomable abyss of language. It begins as the title of a text written in 1935, the most immediate rendition of an experience of, I might say, reality. It consists, as you will recall, of three parts: the rendition of (the) experience itself, its interpretation, that is, the effort to make sense of it, and third, two of what Hannah Arendt calls "poetic" or "cognitive forms" into which the "in principle infinite" interpretation has to be "banned" (disciplined? exiled? caught?—if "caught," "banned" has far more the sense of imprisoned than of caught in the net, as the catch, of "surrender," which I have recognized *Vorgang* as the most path-setting among my earliest experiences of the kind). And I would not use the word "banned" as the form into which the unending interpretation could be forced, but rather a hapless word such as transformed or metamorphosized, to cover the ignorance of what occurs or occurred. Or so I felt about the last two pieces of *Vorgang*, "Dreamward" and "Snake Arms," where I sketched or painted the most horrible fate of man, which become known as Auschwitz. These last two pieces, "poetic" or "cognitive forms" in Arendt's terms, were intrinsic and inextricable parts of the catch which I call *Vorgang*, and which consisted of its three parts.

Vorgang—that which goes forth, goes on—begins thus (to remember):

Face to face: there stands the word. Face to face the sea, separated from me by hardly three rooms, face to face with me that pure hall, the clarity of which makes shiver and yet smiles at me, but I am swerving so that some words are determined by the swerve of the beautiful letter; did I not love the smoothness of the "R," it would perhaps not have come to "by three rooms," but in the drunkenness after all the swerve really becomes the word, lust becomes validity, the very unique—the word which stands there against every reflection—readable. Reeling, lovingest seeing, seeing into the sea, above the sea: it clears wide under my window, reeling with which I am alone, with which alone I can be if I am myself.

Call on me, how should it not come out of the deepest wine jugs what in the years fermented in the sea and filled the drunkenness from which I was far away? Pour, I am holding the glass, deep, and it presses against all clarity of the sea, which begins at the mountain's spread and knows that the dark drink blesses the tides.

I feel transferred into the midst of that experience, and yet I also feel in need of getting out of it. First, into an observation concerning the translatability of the beginning of *Vorgang* just presented again. For a very long time, it seems forever, I had thought the translation of *Vorgang* would be hopeless. I would secretly, as it were, go into details of what I thought was impossible to render in a different language, but I now translated it rather quickly and easily. I'm not clear about the nature of this change but suspect the continued thought concerning the nature of surrender-and-catch has made this idea and its expression somewhat less difficult to handle. A second thing I want to touch on in getting out of the experience rendered in the quotation is a comparison of the transformations of interpretations of interpretation into a "poetic or cognitive form" with certain final solutions—what a horrible term! but may it here be used in all objectivity—in music; two are the ones I am thinking of in particular: the end of Ravel's *Bolero* and the end of Gershwin's *Rhapsody in Blue*, in both of which it is as if the whole orchestra were called upon finally to resolve the theme the composer could not get otherwise out of than in this almost violent, imposed way, which more nearly "bans," abolishes, finishes the ever-rising theme or tune than a "poetic or cognitive form" could "ban" an interpretation.

But above all, I want to get into a consideration of the word *Vorgang* itself. This word has many meanings, or, perhaps depending on the mood in which it is approached, is a pun. *Vorgang* means going before, but it also means going on; *Vorgang* thus means something which is going on, a process (from pro-cessus, that is, *Vorgang*) or event (from ex-venire, to come out), thus *Vorgang* as the title of the text could be translated as "Event" or

"Process," something which happens or happened. But its composition of three parts also indicates what it is that is going on: an, as it were, overwhelming text, the effort to make sense of it, and the catch of this sense, the sense caught, as the shudder of humanity's future. But then I end the whole with this sentence: "With the cloth of shame I covered my face and passed on." I suddenly changed into a person to whom something had happened, something for which he was not responsible but of which he nevertheless felt ashamed and left the scene of the *Vorgang*, or wanted to leave it, as if this could make any difference in this moral play, which was deeper than interpretation; it was a play of responsibility.

Thus it turns out that the problem of *Vorgang* is not so much the "in principle unending interpretation" as the interaction between interpretation and moral responsibility. It looks as if the interpretation were unending only if its moral component is ignored. In reality, however, there is an awareness, no matter how subdued, that the interpretation shapes what it interprets, that is, the world, in its image and that this defining of the world is not only a cognitive but also a moral act, for which I, unaware of it, want to exculpate myself.

If this is so, the interpretation is not "in principle unending" until the interpreter's life ends, but until it becomes aware of its own moral responsibility or action. Thus the "in principle unendable" interpretation is not "banned" into a "poetic or cognitive form" but, so to speak, comes into its own in such a "form."

This recognition of the moral dimension or nature of interpretation is an unexpected demonstration of the fact that in surrender, received notions—here the ordinarily taken-for-granted distinction between interpretation and moral judgment—are suspended. In the present instance, the catch, or a catch, of surrendering to an analysis of certain aspects of the first paragraph of *Vorgang* is the moral character of interpretation; in other words, the result of the suspension of the distinction between interpretation and moral judgment has been the affirmation of the coexistence of both in interpretation—but we might add, in moral judgment as well, since every moral judgment also is an interpretation. Interpretation and moral judgment in their coexistence have stood the test of surrender.

We have been talking about some views of how a process ends. But how does it begin? Somewhere, I think in *The Human Condition*, Arendt refers to Saint Augustine as having said that human beings are the beings who can begin things, I suppose by virtue of the creativity implanted by God in his children. But how, if at all, does such an explanation apply to the beginning of a piece of writing? We have seen in *Vorgang* a text impress itself on me, or rather, what impressed itself on me was what turned out to be the beginning, the *Anfang*, the "initial catch." Such a degree as here to which things are not taken for granted is unusual: what it is characterized by, as I came later to put it, is an unusually high degree of the suspension of received notions, as experience of surrender, a leaving or transcendence of the world of everyday life in which tables are tables, people have names, and they can be called by telephone. In many more texts, the world of everyday life remains as the scene of action and reflection as does the world of science in a scientific paper or that of history in a historical one, etc.: in the beginning of the text there generally is a problem within one of these worlds.

I wonder whether my claim earlier in these pages on Hannah Arendt's letter that an interpretation of it, or already the effort to translate it from the German, would lead to the "abyss of language" was a feeling by now replaced by the analysis of "with the cloth of shame I covered my face and passed on" and the clarification of the moral component of interpretation. If this were the case we would once more be saved from the opening or closing into insanity. But this would not mean, as Hannah Arendt suggests, that one could keep on interpreting one's interpretations *ad infinitum*, where this *infinitum* would be one's death, but that on another occasion of surrender—to whatever or whomever that might be—the "abyss of language" could not be clarified.

Now to Hermann Broch's "remarks" on *Vorgang*.

Sunday, 8 November '98, 16:24

I feel unsure of why I recorded the date and the hour, even the minute, when I sat down to type; perhaps it symbolizes my desire of a fixed point, as external to me as it may seem—but in reality it only does seem that way. In reality it is as much a part of me as the thoughts I'll try to formulate, thoughts about Hermann Broch's "remarks." Still, I have the vague but very pulsating feeling that I have to start all over again. To start, that is, my attempt to understand *Vorgang* and its meaning in my life. Of course, I think, it was a case of surrender, which changed my life, shaping it, but how and in what sense and direction? Before *Vorgang* I took myself for granted as a poet and writer, who had to write whatever he had to, without an overall plan. After *Vorgang*—though I took decades to become aware of what had taken place—I have been devoted to exploring and applying the idea of surrender-and-catch. The present text is the latest phase of this exploration. At this stage in this latest phase, there now follows a second comment on *Vorgang*, even though it was written in 1948, more than nine years earlier than Hannah Arendt's. The reason that it follows her rather than having its chronological place is that this whole project started with my curiosity about Hannah Arendt's comment and developed from it.

Here, then, are, in my translation from the German.

Remarks on *Vorgang* by Kurt H. Wolff[2]

By Hermann Broch

This rational poem—one can't call it anything else—was written in 1935. That is a strange fact, for in it a purely existentialist attitude is taken, and at that time existentialism had not yet been invented.

The attempt is to bring about, so to speak, a primordial relation between subject and object in observing the relation in its various phases, that is, in its various media. These media show themselves as those of language and the superlinguistic conceptual structure on the one hand, and the sense impressions on the other.

It may be said, with some simplification, that for the presentation a fundamental cross of coordinates is laid down. Along one of the coordinates (horizontal) the process of cognition or, briefly, the *Vorgang*, is portrayed in its progressing from sense impression to concept, respectively in its regression from concept to sense impression, which now is identified with the "word" and thus is lifted into the medium of language. By contrast on the second (vertical) coordinate the whole (horizontal) process is, so to speak, made into a sense impression, that is, is itself in turn being observed and portrayed. It goes without saying that the method could and should be continued; the whole of the two rows of portraits should now be portrayed along a third coordinate (sounding lead). In short, there is an urge toward n-dimensional poetry.

With this the existential enterprise is undertaken much more seriously than the existentialists have ever done it. It is a wholly new approach to poetry, entirely original; it is not to be compared with the method of Joyce, although Joyce too took aim at multidimensionality.

An ever further addition of new dimensions of portrayal, however, is impossible both technically and poetically. Somewhere there must be a stop. Here the author lets two coordinates be enough. The portrait lines along coordinates 3 to n remain unused; even as it is, it is complicated enough.

In other words, in every presentation, and thus in this one, too, a point must be reached where the naive confidence in the natural word enters. Speaking logically, the point where formalization is broken off and the rule of operation must be given with natural words.

It is the point where in poetry, real, that is, lyrical poetry enters. It is the gift of the artist (who at the core is always a lyricist, must be a lyricist) to be able to put together the missing dimensions, n^1 to infinity, in a single symbol, no matter whether this takes place already at n^1 or n^2 or later somewhere else. A method like that of *Vorgang* shows that poetic knowledge must no longer as it once did stop at n^1 if it wants to be honest (perhaps later it will again return to the old method); still, the lyrical demand remains. Or, putting it more precisely, every work of art is up to a certain point a rational statement, no matter how subtly resolved the statement may be, yet what remains of the unresolvable can only be expressed lyrically.

This additional lyrical poetry of the irrational is in my opinion not contained in the piece under discussion. In view of the youth of the author (13 years ago) this is also understandable; he was much too taken by the discovery of his new poetic method to be able to get very far beyond it. To be sure, he sensed that something was missing; he also tried to go beyond it, the lyricism is replaced above all by the philosophical, that is, by a kind of thought lyricism; but this lyricism itself remains in the rational sphere, the attempt is made to romanticize it so that in this fashion an approximation to the irrational may succeed. Such romantic irrationalizations lie, for instance, in the sexualization of the *Vorgang*; the identification of drunkenness-primordial-sensation-discharge-of-semen belong in this category. However, not only is this fundamentally too primitive, too youthfully primitive, the breakthrough to the lyrical is not achieved and cannot be achieved; Joyce, too, far more complex, far more worked through, shows this.

This lack has its effect above all as lack of any tension; since there is no summing up, and the philosophical summing up won't do, the overall structure, despite its seeming density, ultimately remains loose, a conglomerate. It becomes in a certain way surrealistic; that is, it becomes a structure the major effect of which lies in details which in conglomerating try to move away from each other. A painting by Breughel has tension because it is held together in an irrational perspective, whereas a Dali in its rationality remains completely without tension, and to a certain degree this is so here, too. Surely there is no art without certain schizoid roots, but surrealism believes that it already produces art when it shows the schizoid.

Summarizing, it can be said that here is a work which is highly significant for modern poetry because it represents in great honesty and with extraordinary intensity a new approach to new levels of reality. The author, however, is at the beginning of a road which must first be dug up and walked on; only then can there be hope to find primordial symbols such as are sought here.

This was written on February 7, 1948. In a brief accompanying note, Broch wrote:

> This is my—I stress it—subjective impression. It can only be subjective, for the chasm between generations means (as I already said clearly) a difference of apperception schemes.

Seven months later, on September 8, 1948, Broch wrote:

> Our letters crossed each other . . . this one emphasizes a very beautiful and important moment of your poetic position, the attempt at gaining an absolute point zero from which poetry is to begin, that is, the continuous renewed stress of the word together with the object presented. I don't know whether this is also contained in my 'assessment' [the "Remarks" above]; at any rate it belongs there.
>
> I consider this an unresolvable antinomy, as the antinomy of pulling-oneself-up-by-one's-braid. But it is the basic antinomy of all philosophizing, and what philosophy is, and must be, allowed must also be allowed to poetry. On the contrary, it is high time that poetry become in this sense finally really philosophical. After all, Joyce, too, has tried similar things. Only there is nevertheless a fundamental difference; philosophy will for this very reason mathematize itself more and more whereas poetry cannot do this but rather, in consequence of its lyrical nature [*Gehalts*], remain bound to "content."

1

This is quite an onslaught. But—the first thing Hermann Broch does, as if fighting off the onslaught of *Vorgang*, is to categorize it, calling it a "rational poem" in which "a purely existentialist attitude is taken" and at a time existentialism had not yet been invented.

I am, of course, proud of having been able to interest such important writers as Hannah Arendt and Hermann Broch to the point of making them write and write what they did. And I like *Vorgang* being labeled a rational poem, by which I take it Broch means the remainder of his remarks to be an explication of. The core of the meaning of "rational poem" is the effort to bring about a "primordial relation between subject and object." Broch skips the question of what subject or object are by pointing out that this relation is sought—to simplify somewhat—by observing the relations between language and sense impressions.

2

I interrupt here, possibly affected by Hermann Broch in the desire to categorize. What is it that Broch is doing? What does *Remarks* (*Bemerkungen*) mean? Do they constitute a commentary? An interpretation? I now find it strange that such a question never came up in regard to Hannah Arendt's letter about *Vorgang*—because it *is* a letter, requiring no classification other than that? At any rate, I must now ask about the meaning, that is, the etymology of the terms mentioned.

Bemerkung means pretty much the same as "remark" and has the same origin, having to do with "mark" (*Marke*); a remark is the expression of something noticed, perceived, one is aware of, etc. A *commentary* (from the Latin *comminisci*, "to contrive by thought") is a series of comments or explanations or interpretations. An *interpretation*, finally (from the act or work of an interpreter), is, in nontechnical, popular language, an explanation.³

"Remarks" strikes me as far too modest a title of what Broch actually writes, which is more nearly a theory of *Vorgang*, a viewing or contemplating (from *thea*). For reasons I do not know, he uses metaphors such as a mathematician or engineer might use (had he been one before he became a writer in his mature adulthood? I don't want to interrupt again to find out); he structures my effort along two coordinates which, however, change—and here his poetic vein beats—in a kind of Hegelian dialectic: on one coordinate we find the movement from sense impression to concept (and vice versa); on the other, this whole movement as a sense impression—which could and should go on to a third coordinate. This suggestion parallels Hannah Arendt's "in principle" unendable interpretation (I don't know whether she knew Broch's essay); let us see how Broch's comment continues.

More than two "dimensions" than those of the two coordinates, he writes, are "impossible both technically and poetically." For it is at this point, or so I read Broch, "where the naive confidence in the natural word enters." Unless I don't understand or misunderstand Broch, what he means is that at a certain point in the course of what Broch a little further down refers to as lyrical writing, the language of everyday life puts in its claim of being the language of "paramount reality," preventing, so to speak, the genius from going mad (if it does).

3

I am deeply grateful to Hermann Broch for his recognition of the poetic component—if not nature—of *Vorgang*. The reason he calls it a "rational poem" is, I surmise, my attempt (in "Interpretation") to go as far as I could interpreting and only then turned "lyrical," was "banned" into a "poetic or cognitive form." But I don't achieve the breakthrough into the lyrical; instead, I turn in my effort to reach the irrational, for instance, to equaling "drunken, primordial sensation, and discharge of semen." Broch excuses me because of my youth and because I "was too much taken by . . . my new poetic method to be able to get far beyond it." As to the lack of tension, I must disagree, I do feel tensions between different pieces of the text. Neither can I agree with the absence of tension in Dali (except for his last phase of "religious" paintings). But in his accompanying note, Broch relativizes much of his criticism as being an expression of a generation gap. In the other letter, he gives his opinion about poetry and philosophy: philosophy will increasingly mathematize itself (influence of the Vienna Circle on Broch?), which poetry cannot because, being lyrical, it is inseparable from content. (It is as if Broch compared mathematics, rather than philosophy, with poetry.)

But just before this diagnosis and prognosis, he writes something of great importance and consequences about my effort:

> to gain an absolute point zero from which poetry is to begin, that is, the continuous renewed stress of the word together with the object presented. . . . I consider this an unresolvable antinomy of pulling-oneself-up-by-one's-braid. But it is the basic antimony of all philosophizing, and . . . must be allowed to poetry . . . it is high time that poetry become in this sense really philosophical.

As far as I can make this out, the unresolvable dichotomy is between the desire to reach that point zero and the impossibility of reaching it. This is the point where poetry begins, this is, when "the continued renewed stress of the word together with the object presented" begins, that is, where language begins.

Yes, and bravo, and thank you, Hermann Broch! For without using the word "surrender"—it was two years before it occurred to me and decades, as I said, before I recognized *Vorgang* as an instance of it—Hermann Broch points out that no matter how hard we try, we cannot create poetry or philosophy because language is already there before we are. Language is the human instrument for dealing with everything in all ways that language has at its and thus our disposal, including, but not limited to, poetry and philosophy. Even the most radical surrender imaginable can do no more than speak more correctly than was possible before it occurred, since it simply cannot do without language. (Not that I know whether Hermann Broch would agree with this formulation.)

How does this compare with what it says about the abyss of language at the end of the discussion of Hannah Arendt's letter about *Vorgang*? There the *infinitum* of interpretation showed itself to be ended by the recognition, generally and case by case concretely, of the moral dimension of interpretation. In the discussion of Hermann Broch's *Remarks*, what was at issue was not the unendability of interpretation but the no more than relative absoluteness of surrender, its limitation by language.

The moral nature of interpretation and the limit set on surrender by language are the two main things I have learned by surrendering to these two writings, by Hannah Arendt and Hermann Broch. These thus are the two main things I have learned in this fashion about *Vorgang* and its meaning in my life.

A Letter to Hermann Broch[4]

This may be a good point at which to present (translated from the German) a letter I wrote to Hermann Broch on the occasion of the first publication of *Vorgang* in 1978, twenty-seven years after Broch's death (and one year before the publication of *Surrender and Catch*, the basic and opening book on the topic).

Newton, Mass., January 12, 1976

Beloved and revered Hermann Broch,

   In the meantime it is 1976, I am a bit older than you were at the time of the "Remarks on *Vorgang*," and moved to where now the abyss between generations lives on in case it does I don't know—I surely feel it in myself too. Although I haven't changed much in the revision of *Vorgang*, after the second world war and the partly bureaucratically planned, partly panicky, partly panickily planned, panicky according-to-plan wounding, torturing, annihilation of millions of people, *Vorgang* looks different. Do you know what after more than forty years reminded me of it again, made me look at it once again and then read it again, to bring it with your "Remarks" to its feet, now to write my own interpretation and as a letter to you? A film on the life of the Jews in Nazi-infected Holland (and on devout Christians)! It was unbearable as ever, and there was personal anguish. Where then were my chances, what were the chances of humanity? It was a relief—no, don't laugh—when I remembered, even if only vaguely, the last pages of *Vorgang*, "on cliffs you will have to live," wrongly quoted from the second part of Dreamward, "It will be different and much worse, you will have to live on cliffs and on boulders, needle-pointed, so that your feet would hurt if you could walk, but you cannot walk . . . the rock splinter penetrates you constantly; when it crackles in the air it is death . . ."; and then "On this shark you'll have to live, my mouth was saying while my heart was being torn . . ., glad of the scale which will be your house, your hold a tiny pointed growth, beloved thorns and the near hasty red joy and dizziness to your eyes, without food, without work you last out until the giant, shaking, throws you before his throat—when you move it is destruction, and only through your death will you feed the fish who now can be caught no longer." And I? In the face of this horrible expectation— what did I do? I saved my life already in this prediction itself, in this vision, which was so unbearable that it whispers only in images, imagingly hisses, I "snaked" myself, though not toward the "ray and shark sea to live in it," but "winding myself, wonder-swelled": not quite four years later I fled, out of the beloved, Nazi-run Italy, winding, skillfully wonder-swelled also by what had entered me, what I saw ("prophet" whom nobody heard)—but since then ununderstanding and guilty, trying to forget the feeling guilty—because my life and the fight against the Nazis, against all enemies of man, against all evil is not one and the same—by fleeing into that which "I must really do, must eventually still do, what I am here for"; to feel that I don't have to feel guilty.

I really believe that I already then connected the two last sections of *Vorgang*, "Dreamward" and "Snake Arms," with the political breakdown of Europe, with the political bankruptcy. "Bankruptcy" is the right word: in addition to enthusiasm and the poetical there was cynicism—that is, I was as unpolitical as these two sections are if they are taken literally, not to mention what precedes them: my imagination was concerned with a world that was hopeless, ripe, like a taut ulcer for nothing but tender poetic caressing. To save—nothing! But after all, one could act as if one counted on the spirit—of its blowing could no longer be any talk—subterraneously still creeping about, probably neighing with totally noiseless irony, so that it would spit out the human madness which had infected it. You write that "the single symbol" "in which the artist" puts together "the missing dimensions," this "arch symbol" is missing. I see *Vorgang* differently, at least now; I believe it is clearer than it was why I can say it now more clearly. Surely there is the search for the word, for the believable because ineluctable, including what you call the philosophical, but the seeker stops the search and instead is satisfied, finds home, comes to rest in the "full doing" of Dreamward and Snake Arms. And I just pointed to what satisfies this full doing in the most terrible visions and where they come from. This means that at this moment in the history of mankind the analysis of poetry and philosophy and their relation struck me as frivolous, was over, or at least was not what was found or was not yet found. Ever again the guilt, so that *Vorgang* stops with the beginning-end, the end-beginning: "With the cloth of shame I covered my face and moved on": forget me, forgive me, I don't know myself, no, I have never been here, at most may what I thought lie about there or there.

You write, and in a different sense does Hannah Arendt, that *Vorgang* is a beginning. I am glad, you are right!

[A detailed report follows, making up more than the second half of the letter, on the meaning, in English and German, of "surrender-and-catch" and how it developed since 1950. I end in a mood, in which I refer to Suzuki, Husserl, and Agee as self-confessed beginners, and concluding as follows.] Now then when I end, I feel beginning and embrace you, as ever, as never, as always.

Yours,
Kurt

How am I to continue? I am writing this much later than what here precedes, having had forgotten that I made two main points of my letter: guilt and the political-historical place of surrender-and-catch: they both go back much farther than I realized. But let a psychoanalyst come to terms with this if one of them is sufficiently enamored of his or her work and has nothing better to do. I continue with what I have written already, looking for repetitions to excise, connections to explicate, and other improvements to make.

Notes

1. This letter was published in the original German in *Vorgang und immerwährende Revolution*, (Wiesbaden: Heymann, 1978), 50, and in *Sozialwissenschaften als Kunst*, edited by Peter Ludes (Konstanz: Universitatsverlag, 1997), 199.

2. Here translated from the original typescript; published as "Bemerkungen zu 'Vorgang' von Kurt [H.] Wolff" (1948) in *Scnriften zur Literatur, I, Kritik*, edited by Hermann Broch, (Kommentierte Werkausgabe, Band 9/1), (Frankfurt am Main: Suhrkamp, 1975), 398–401. Previously also published in *Vorgang und immerwährend Revolution*, 47–50, and in *Sozialwissenschaften als Kunst*, 189–92.

3. See Friedrich Kluge, *Etymologisches Wörterbuch der deutschen Sprache*, 16th ed., edited by Walther Nitzka (Berlin 1960); and *The American Heritage Dictionary of the English Language*, 1969.

4. This letter was published in *Vorgang und immerwährende Revolution*, 51–55, and again in *Sozialwissenschaften als Kunst*, 193–97.

CHAPTER 4

Another Beginning

1

O yes there is more than one way to begin but the O yes (almost sounding "O Yes!") did it. Did what? Well, make the beginning because it injects hopes has given hope. I am beginning. "But you have done it," I heard from his blue-gray eyes, his fishskin-colored eyes besides which no skin, dirty white as it would probably have been, mattered, could have mattered. But "*it*"? What "it"? As soon as this question formulated itself I was overcome with a shower of blessing: "it" was the work of my life, I had written my work.

What was it? It was a song of sixpence, quite happy, it was paradise, intermittently found, I could hardly look, the sun was so bright, but his fishskin-colored eyes relieved me of my task, made me free finally, at the end of life, to write what would, what would be written, what would write. What? What trust now.

2

Suddenly there is a number 2. The relation to what now appears as the preceding? I didn't think of looking at what I had written; I was to add, not relate, to it. But that was when I knew what was to be next: about the spirit, which was somehow at stake, at issue. Somehow it had been stripped—I don't know of what; the spirit was what it all boiled down to, but I have forgotten. So I didn't know how to go on, and yet something had started and wanted more. Thus I wanted to look at what it was, what was written, so to see what it demanded.

I rested, I was exhausted. It came back as soon as I closed my eyes: It was the spirit exhausted, driven to its utmost—spirit, but what was the spirit? What was that which didn't let me rest but smashed me to continue asking, asking? Of course I was exhausted, perhaps engaged in endless interpretation of the just-interpreted, with no resolution, solution, absolution, no telling what's what so I would know. As it is, I don't know, I am in suspense.

3

I haven't read anything I wrote before; I'd probably be surprised by at least some of it. The river keeps on flowing by the terrace, noising as ever and always, but tonight I have met a woman from my native town, my native town, my native street, the house number where the destroyed post office used to stand, Darmstadt, Rheinstrasse 1, her name the same as that of a good youth friend, by now a long-retired Washington bureaucrat, no she didn't know him, and why do I write all this, is it only because she has Parkinson's, am I infected as if by the river's water? Too tired to explore (further).

4

But something is—feels, I feel, it is or was as if there was a hole in the rug, more even, as if I had made a hole into the rug by punching a blunt instrument, a short, sharp-pointed pair of scissors through the carpet and saw the bottom but right away knew it's not the bottom but only another surface, unsmoother than the one I stand on, blowsily blistering like the skin of a shrunken egg, under which there are innumerable surfaces, smooth or unsmooth it doesn't matter since there is no end to depth, or surface for that matter, except sleep.

5

No, I haven't regained my foothold in the everyday world, the "paramount reality." Is it because I am in the process of discovering that it isn't really paramount but only imposed on us by our bodies? This sounds eminently Eastern, and suddenly the word *maya*, or something like it, which I had stamped out of my memory for probably decades, came back: as the foam in which we are engulfed. And yet I persist on claiming that, "surrender-and-catch" is a *Western* idea because the catch, rather than surrender, is its telos, while in the Eastern version surrender is. Perhaps one could say that in the idea of surrender-and-catch it is *Ocupo* that supercedes *mi preocupo* while in the East *preocupo* obliterates all activity. Most important may be the fact that in the East the *Lebenswelt* is so to speak written off, whereas surrender looks at it searchingly as raising as many questions as any world does, thus inventing and developing, among many other things, social science, which with the elevation of the *Lebenswelt* to the paramount reality has become blind to its potential and thus needs new surrender to it. On surrender-and-catch as a Western or a universally human idea, see, however, chapter 7, sections 14 to 17, and especially 18.

6

The sinking sun framed the window—of course you would have put it the other way around, the window framed the sun, since the window is or has a frame, not the sun: the sun is round and thus cannot serve as a frame, but I try to write faithfully, and the window was in the middle of the sun, which thus framed it and framed a lot more. Which made me feel good: I could truthfully describe it, I even had to. I also felt similarly better because Clara phoned, to thank me for sending her a paper, which she called considerate, also announcing that she expected a baby, when, in December, also asking how I was and what I was doing, she would call again another time. Perhaps the absence of hate or indifference along with having rested.

7

Is all that happened a shift from Loma to *Vorgang*? Is "all" all of the events, feelings, thoughts of the last days of my life? Or is "all" the same as "no more than?" Or do the two coincide? Look at the original question in either reading: it is a question of interpretation, of meaning. What is the meaning of this shift, from Loma to *Vorgang*, and separately but inseparably, what is its significance? First, we must clarify some of the terms composing the question, that is, "Loma," "*Vorgang*," and "shift" (from Loma to *Vorgang*).

8

"*Vorgang*" is easier to present than "Loma" or "shift." It is, to begin with, a typescript of some fifty to seventy pages, depending on the size of the type and the margins, written in a short period of time in the summer of 1935 in Camogli (near Genoa) through a window above the Mediterranean, in the blinding, enlightening-clarifying love of my beloved (who was to become my wife a year later and to remain my wife until she died in 1990) and in the love of the world and all that is in it. It was a time of glory, into which fell a text and its interpretation, an event, a process, a *Vorgang*, which I recognized only decades later as an instance of surrender-and-catch: I had surrendered to my being when and where I was and as directly as I could "worded" it or (same thing) as it came. In that surrender, in still other words, there produced itself the "catch," the harvest, yield, product of surrender, that is, the written *Vorgang*, and so much that followed, including the idea of surrender-and-catch and the many pages about it, and "Loma."

Loma is a place or, by now, *was* a place (with a different name in the everyday world) where—I notice I've never so put it before—everyone of the about two hundred Lomans knew every house and everyone who lived in every house and you gave direction by residents and their houses rather than by streets, of which there was hardly more than one.

This was the place where something happened, happened to me: my research plan fell flat to the ground because I had fallen in love with Loma and the Lomans and with myself-in-Loma, with my moment there. What was there? What was I doing there? It was a big question, I was a big question, but I didn't think even of asking, much less answering it; instead, the question was directed at everything I could observe and remember and record; I was as if obsessed by wanting-to-know, drunk with the confidence that I would find out. What I'd find out, as I came to formulate it six years later, was the catch of my surrender.

Thus Loma is not simply a place, not even simply a place where I experienced surrender but also, or it has become also, a process, a *Vorgang*, an instance of surrender-and-catch, with the catch far less "in" than I had thought when I drafted several earlier versions of "the study of Loma." Those versions were aimed at developing the idea of surrender-and-catch by using the material I had collected in and on Loma. Now I feel freed from this task, just having delivered the gist of the meaning of Loma, namely, in relation to *Vorgang*. Now then to the question of the meaning and the significance of the shift from Loma to *Vorgang*.

9

But something has happened. I thought and still think that I had written a few pages in an exploratory mood like these, but could not find them, either in memory or in the external world. Then this morning I suddenly remembered (I don't recall what led to it) blue-gray, fishskin-colored eyes, the eyes of that color, then the reassuring words that I had done "it" already. This must have been the beginning of those pages that wouldn't let themselves be found, and I was relieved, as well as disturbed by my unbelievably defective memory—which I still don't want to trust, prepared for those pages to turn up in memory and, perhaps, then materially. But I do remember and relive the glory documented in what I am supposed to believe is the first paragraph of the present pages. How did they go on, how are they going on?

10

The everyday answer comes from reading what precedes. But this would not disclose the connection, other than literal, of the pages read, the connection between *Vorgang* and Loma. It occurred to me only today that some sort of good society must have played a role: in *Vorgang* the world was beautiful and lovable, and in Loma I was contented with the world, notwithstanding criticism. What is even more compelling about the significance of connecting the two, *Vorgang* and Loma, is that I had written, during the summer of 1933, two years before *Vorgang*, a novel, *Organda* (the last thing I wrote before leaving Nazi Germany), in which I contrast my daily life with its people, adored and despised, and a society across the border where people lived a simple if cruel life, as I fancied it, a life severely regulated by laws, particularly threats and punishments. My picture of that society echoed the incipient totalitarianism in Germany, in its cruelty and in its fascination. In fact, one of the questions that preoccupied me at that time was how to live with Nazism as a Jew; my thought resulted in an essay, which, I remember astonished and embarrassed by my ignorance, argued for the compatibility of the two. But the longing for the good society whatever that means, has remained, and tears come to my eyes when I remember old Patricia in Loma rolling with her beautiful, dry fingers a cigarette under her beautiful face. Thus Loma remains to this day a memory of beauty despite its many miseries which in fact led to its end, foredoomed as it was when by now more than ninety years ago, the establishment of a national forest deprived it of its grazing ground for the sheep and forced an ever increasing number of Lomans to seek first seasonal and then ever more permanent work outside Loma: by the last time I was there, in 1974, emigration and, of course, death, had left just a few original Lomans. They had been replaced by outsiders who had modernized existing houses or built their own to go fishing in the nearby Red River in the summer or skiing in the winter or simply enjoying the beauty of the landscape.

My longing for the good society has been documented at least since an even earlier piece, "The Everlasting Revolution" ("Die immerwahrende

Revolution"[1]), which records a mysterious, continuous effort to improve society, and this longing has become enormously stronger with the unfolding not only of Nazism and totalitarianism elsewhere but also of bureaucratization and, altogether, the violent suppression of reason other than in its technical, mean-end, functional sense, that is, the identification of reason with efficiency and the disappearance of its substantive nature. Thus the ever more preponderant emphasis on the *historical* importance of the idea of surrender-and-catch, rather than on that as which it had shown itself to me originally: as a critical experience.

11

I am thinking of the river rushing by across the hall. I am thinking of how different this rushing is from people's rushing, including my own. My rushing is a mixture of the two, the river's and people's. For instance, I did not know that I would write what I just wrote or that this would be the point where I did. I was free of the rushing of the day, of "people's" rushing, I could again trust the rushing of my undertaking, which continued to be to uncover the relations between *Vorgang* and Loma and, indeed, my life: What does "my life" mean? Is it no more than satisfying the demands of body and soul, that is, of the two components of the human being that make it a "mixed phenomenon," one that has features shared with other contents of the cosmos, from stones to chimpanzees, from volume and weight to language, and features which are exclusively human—philosophy, poetry, science, art, in one word, the unending and unendable search for meaning? I ask again: can I say that the meaning of my life is to satisfy these demands? I don't want to answer "yes" for fear of risking my autonomy. I should rather entrust my autonomy to myself, to a task I have, because I am who I am, however much I share with some and all other human beings. I do not know where I got this idea of a task, even a mission from, but it is very old and has hardly ever been shaken. By now I can point to a number of its manifestations, above all writings, paintings, and drawings, which I trust or at least hope will survive me, and if only as the legacy of a self-obsessed fool.

12

Since I wrote this, or rather, dictated it, things have changed again. As I was talking about my task or mission I felt like the self-obsessed fool I mentioned at the end. But when I read the text I had in fact dictated I felt relieved by the thought that there was nothing wrong, or "self-obsessed," or foolish in having a task or mission and being aware and proud of it. It had nothing to do with arrogance; it rather was a sign of devotion and purpose. I am and can be without a bad conscience, at peace with my task.

In the meantime I was taken by a friend for a cup of coffee and piece of pastry. Again, and even more inescapably than ever before the world was a stage: people played roles in a setting, in front of houses and stores, walking under trees, a church nearby, people inconspicuously wearing their clothes, displaying parts of their bodies, people calling each other, sometimes being answered, sometimes not. I sat there at a small round table, a swallow of espresso from time to time, in between falling back into watching the stage. Where was I? The place of the cafe in which I sat had a name, but the name was a part of the stage, as were the names, whether I knew them or not, and in fact I don't know that I knew any of the people whom I could see. As so often I looked for the real name.

What is the real name? What is my real name? I discover that these are two quite different questions. I should think that the answer to the first, concerning the "real name" of things other than myself, is a problem of historical semantics. But historical semantics covers only one aspect of the real name of a person: its family history, for example, the naming of the newborn after a grandfather or because of personal taste. It covers the everyday history of naming, that feature of naming which people share with the naming of other human features. But it does not concern that meaning which applies to the human being exclusively. For all I know, this is a nameless name since its bearer would not be burdened by it in his or her movements, in his or her essential life. It is like the name of God in Judaism which must not be pronounced or written—just as the Roman emperor driven by his curiosity concerning the "Jewish secret," broke open the holy of holies and found that it contained nothing. When it comes to the knowledge of things themselves we must give up all hope because the only access to them is by means of the cognitive equipment without which we could grasp nothing but which tells us how to look at things, that is, our knowledge of things results from the interaction between us and them. (This does not mean that there are no universal features in all processes of socialization without the assumption of which we could not account for the possibility of translation in the broadest sense of the term, including that from one language to another, the study of history, anthropology, psychology, etc.)

13

I'd have to reread the preceding section to see how I got into an epistemological discussion, but I remember without checking that it was from the world as a stage to everyday versus "real" names which, understood as the names of things in themselves as we cannot know, for—to put the reason for this in another way—we ourselves are of the world in which we are born, live a while, and die. The world as a stage was an impression, a sensation; thus the question how to get behind its wings and the answer with which I was familiar and comfortable.

But not content, the answer was and had become for me a tradition, hence must be suspended. But no matter how hard I think about it, I cannot come up with a better answer. Still, I am not surrendering to it; the question is not fully "face to face" with me (*gegenuber*); it came up, is tangential to my still prevailing concern, the meaning and significance, for me and I hope and believe for others, of "Vorgang" and "Loma" and their relation. Thus the place of the question concerning "real" names, things themselves, is different from that directed to a Sister in the discussion of her paper on surrender and prayer as to whether she could suspend her faith in Jesus Christ: I have always interpreted her thoughtful negative answer as expressing the point beyond which she could not surrender, presumably having imagined as unrestricted an effort to do so as she could. Not so, obviously, here.

14

But then came Mamma Pacchetto. In a dream, not to confuse you. I was chatting I don't remember what about, but probably something past, with newly found friends (visited? Why not earlier when more of them would have been still alive?), sprawled on the ground of some street-crossing near houses: I remember only Antonia, the domineering younger sister of Cecilia the beauty compared with whom Antonia had no beauty, no features, only a continually snapping voice, aiming at victory over Cecilia's flame of Venetian—or Ruben—red hair which you, astonished but full of approval as you were bound to be, could observe her balancing by her graceful gait. Cecilia had long before my visit died, but her and Antonia's mother and sixty years ago also Carla's and my mother, the mother of us all, was still alive because, or so it must have been, she couldn't leave her kitchen, the center of her life and, indeed, of ours. "The house right in front of you," Antonia said and pointed straight ahead, but first we couldn't see any house right in front of us, only a gap ("we" included Carla, who had of course joined our group or was a member of it from the beginning), then what looked like the temporary cardboard cover, covered in turn with a sparsely patterned oilcloth, green on white, but Antonia's violent nodding toward it made us go there and open the previously invisible door.

It *was* cardboard, and I remember no furniture, only, vaguely, a raw, so to speak naked staircase with, probably, no banister, then a room upstairs in which several unidentifiable voices indicated for us to wait. Soon Mamma Pacchetto emerged through an again invisible door, more leaned over than sitting in a wheelchair, which she herself, 120 or 130 years old that she must be, have been, turned by the wheels. Inspecting her, she was at once recognizable and recognized, changed little from the Mamma Pacchetto of sixty years before. She had grown fatter or at any rate more voluminous, the features of her face had become more real but at the same time less distinct, as if on the way to being lost to the global form out of which they had been carved. But as a whole, Mamma Pacchetto had gained weight, and I was the more astonished when I noticed that she wore shorts, exposing the over-full presence of her thighs, thus giving a surprising comical meaning to her name, Pacchetto. The expression on her face was of pain and anger, but half of her was already no longer there, was gone, was among the dead. She may have spoken, I mean mumbled or tried unsuccessfully to articulate a word or two, but impressed as I was that I still could see her, she was, above all, gone, and I woke up, surprised.

15

Does the connection between *Vorgang* and Loma have at its bottom the good mother? The fact that I just used the bottom metaphor refers to what came up earlier here: that each (really each?) bottom is also a ceiling that can be looked through to uncover a new bottom-ceiling; this is another way of presenting the unfinishability of interpretation except by circumstances external to it, such as loss of interest because of shifting interest, interference with the interpreter (from a neighbor's visit to a disturbing noise to illness to death). Here, however, I'd despite my knowledge and love of Mamma Pacchetto, Patricia and another or two older women and despite Carla's motherly features she developed during our marriage, especially since we became parents—despite all this I feel I know too little about the good mother because, possibly, I didn't consider my own poor mother a good one.

I remember distinctly when I sat on the old sofa on my father's lap and we caressed each other and sang to each other. I remember my contempt—it must have set in soon afterward (when I had been twelve) of "everything" philistine or "bourgeois," including so many of my mother's concerns and worries, such as running from store to store to save a penny on a roll of thread, or her innumerable warnings against improprieties. But my mother was another human being, transfigured, when she was playing the piano—and *that* was what I wanted her to be and wanted to be with her, out of "bourgeois" life into art. And I remember as if it were yesterday rather than seventy-five years ago, how I threw the paisley blanket off the grand piano she was playing around my shoulders and danced, danced guided by the music she was making, the music she after all turned out to *be*. (I also remember one to me of the most inspiring pieces—of which I have long thought nothing—a gavottes by Brahms.)

At this point I want to raise again our basic question: What is the connection between *Vorgang* and Loma? The manifest connection, clearly, which has brought the two together is in the mind: *Vorgang* is an important instance of surrender-and-catch, which I practiced in Loma (without the expression "surrender-and-catch," which came to me only six years later when analyzing what had happened to me in Loma, while the recognition of *Vorgang* as an instance of surrender-and-catch took decades, occurring long after that of Loma. But is there any connection other than in my mind? The only not purely mental one I can think of is the causal connection: something independent of my mind or thought causing *Vorgang*, and/or Loma. But "cause" (as well as "effect") is discovered or defined, that is (once again), is the result of interaction between mind and external world. The difference between causal and cognitive connections is not as profound as might appear at first glance; it is rather like the difference between history and story or fable, fairy tale, novel, and other forms of literature. In causal connections the role (of elements) of the external world is incomparably great than in other connections, that is, interpretations.

I don't know what *caused* the explosion of *Vorgang* other than my happiness and the Mediterranean, as it were, the *mare nostro*. Nor what caused my falling in love with Loma, my compulsive interest in everything there, my impatience with theoretical schemes for studying phenomena "such as" Loma. Could it have had to do with the fact that we had become parents just a few months before and had our baby with us? Nor do I know what "sprang" to "surrender-and-catch" and made the term to stay and develop ever since, close to half a century ago, other than that I was, again, as in the beginning of this development, deeply in love? Nor, finally, do I know what caused the synopsis of *Vorgang* and Loma, that is, why I thought about it for the first time since their existence for sixty and fifty years? I do feel that I just have circumscribed the areas or the area within which to seek the causal connections at issue, but the point here was simply to alert to causal connections as less predominantly cognitive than the one we have pursued. (Also see chapter 5, section 8.)

16

I don't know why I am so jittery, as if my soul were at stake. I did not know how to continue here, lying in bed this morning, very tired but having to get up because of the rules of the house. I began to ponder what would make me get up eventually, and I found that I had no idea. There was a conflict between the gorgeousness of resting and the claim of duty. Which would prevail? I could, after all, have phoned downstairs to ask for breakfast in my room, but this would have meant getting up to the telephone. Thus this was no solution; I would have to get up. The realization of the severe limits of my freedom to act made it easier to act—I did not feel badly enough to entertain the possibility of simply staying in bed. But the conflict between rest and getting up still persisted, and the fact that I would have to get up even to announce that I wouldn't did not eliminate it. It did diminish its violence and made me try to find out how I could respond to the voice of duty: I turned from my back to my side, folded my left elbow, swung my legs over the edge of the bed and, in a kind of unexpected way, was sitting on the edge, almost automatically having slid forward. OK. I'm up, I or it conveyed to myself.

Comment: I did not in this story speak of "deciding" to get up. Even Alfred Schutz, so much more a positivist than I, speaks of a decision as something, which, like a ripe fruit, falls from the tree. I reserve the term "decision" for action on the basis of an examination—within the limits of the actor's range of possibilities —of the actor's available choices. (This highly limited use of the term suggests that "decisions," as well as the expression "I have decided" should be applied far more sparingly than they are.)

But why did I and still do I have this feeling that my soul is at stake, that its fate depends on at least some progress in identifying the process of getting up? Is it the desire to *know* which I present in "Surrender-and-Catch" as a source, perhaps the source, of the desire and necessity to suspend received notions, such as the notion of "deciding to get up"? I am not convinced but rather think that my anxiety is released by the fear of not finding out what getting up means, that is, that I cannot come up with a catch that would make good the claim of the idea of surrender. Still, this is not a satisfactory answer to the question of my anxiousness. For on the other hand I also think that I have sufficiently "delivered the goods" on surrender not to have this fear. I suspect that behind my anxiousness lest I discover something about the process of getting up there lies the anxiety of dying, Schutz's "fundamental anxiety": "I know I must die but I don't want to die." At least not yet, but if and when I should have to suffer physical pain with no or little probability of its ending, I think I would prefer death and in contemplating it would be comforted by what I did manage to write and talk about.

17

I was surprised when I, a short while ago, read what I had dictated yesterday. I had not understood that I had such anxiety, such rather easily accessible anxiety: to unveil it took no more than becoming aware that I didn't know what "getting up" was. Or, more accurately: my becoming aware of my ignorance about getting up made me aware of my overwhelming general ignorance, the ignorance of things, the world, no more intimate, known or even knowable than as a stage. But how I enjoyed this stage (again) this afternoon!

18

I remember waking up this morning that I had left the paper in the machine, interrupting rather than finishing, eager to continue, even though I had forgotten what I had written and was so looking forward to continue. Now, rereading, I do remember: it's the relief of telling simply a story, for the fun of it, without any methodological and epistemological problems such as beset these pages, as if the world had only one bottom and one ceiling, and where the knowledge that this is an illusion doesn't touch on the enjoyment—in which I now wish to indulge.

Once again I saw before me walking in both directions of the sidewalk a delicious collection of figures in the seductive twofold sense of the word "figure," with some of them or parts of them claiming especially commanding attention, partly because of their beautiful or bizarre shape, partly because of their movement. I did not ask what was behind it all, I enjoyed what I saw, not thinking that it was only a surface; had somebody told me so I would have shrugged my shoulders or perhaps smiled compassionately.

But enough of delight. The world as a stage ended up or ends up as not real; it ends up as a pun the key to which has been lost and it escapes from us. What is missing? Words are missing, the right words, words which won't merely "word" our condition, which is dangling between despair and delight. Words which remain; for a very long time I thought they are the poet's words, quoted to myself Novalis's "Was bleibet aber stiften die Dichter" or the English poet's, "The poets are the legislators of humanity" (I may very well not quote accurately); but haven't non-poets, notably philosophers, coined comparable words, for example, Kant's "The sky above and my conscience within me"? What do such words have in common? For one thing they are not everyday speech; in my language they are the catch of surrender to the world (or parts of it); they are spoken in the transcendental world, not in the world of everyday life.

But I seem to be unable to say anything else than what I have just said for the nth time. I don't know whether this means that I cannot surrender to it, that is, be prepared to risk its loss as the catch or part of the catch of this surrender. It would mean living without trust in the transcendental world, being satisfied with the everyday world, the world as a stage, without, of course, seeing it as a stage. This consideration recommends recognition of the existence of the transcendental world next to that of everyday: the idea is that the everyday world has a ceiling which is the bottom of the transcendental world. But this imagery has misled us: it made us forget that the everyday world is our "paramount reality," the realm of interaction other than cognitively, with the external reality, and it is easy therefore to consider the bottom-ceiling theory as applicable, although it may be very difficult to imagine it, to imagine both a world the ceiling of which would be the bottom of the transcendental world and a world the bottom of which would be the ceiling of the transcendental world. These would be, are, no more than vain words, uttered by a busy mouth who has nothing to say.

I am shaken by the turn my writing has taken. I don't know where I am, how I got there, where to go, what for. I must be down to less than my bones; I'm surprised that I am still breathing. Breathing air, air which contains no words. I do need words. Where do I go to get them? I remember, hardly touched by it, surrender, surrender the word maker. I have surrendered. The words lie all around. I am astonished and surprised. Thank you.

19

Thank whom? Thank what for? I am so profoundly grateful that these questions haven't come up. I must, a child, a fool, take it for granted that I am a grateful person the moment I ask myself what I am grateful for, and there is uncountably much, all the way from all things that could be worse but aren't worse, to things that are good or otherwise satisfactory.

And yet I need and I want and I wish or desire, in between satisfaction or the equilibrium of indifference. What the three feelings have in common is a drive for change, but among their differences are the roles of push and pull, the push being most important in the need, the pull most in the desire or wish. By need I mean bodily, physical necessity, or desirability, of which I may not be aware, for example, the need for potassium, or of which I may be keenly aware, for example, hunger, thirst, bladder pressure; in fact, in the last case and some similar ones, the cognitive, emotional self is eliminated, the body takes over. But the same may be said of certain, "compulsory" desires, even though their relation to the body, while obviously important, is more complicated than in the case of hunger; compare my kissing you from an "irresistible" desire to kiss you with my diarrhea.

Wanting, compared with both need and desire, is dominated by cognitive-emotional factors, by the mind. It is of two kinds, depending on what is wanted. What is wanted may be either in the everyday world or in the transcendental world. Examples of the former are "I want to go to school;" "I want to become a banker;" "I want to see this movie;" "I want to make a table." The last example, making, has probably received the most attention, beginning in recent times with Vico, and being discussed in recent decades from the late nineteenth century on, under the misleading label "theory of action" (Pareto, Parsons, Znaniecki, Schutz)—this in an age when very few people produce things by making them but rather by machines, an age where *homo faber* has been increasingly replaced by the job holder, to use Hannah Arendt's term.[2] "Making" follows the means-end scheme; here is my idea of the table I want to make (the end), here are the pieces of wood, etc., I need to make it (means). Following the same scheme, I would say, I want to leave this room (end), therefore I must take the steps to the door (means); my objection to analyzing action, of which, according to the action theorists mentioned, leaving the room is an instance, is that it is hardly descriptive of what typically goes on, if anything, in the mind, of the individual who wants to leave the room. And this to me unrealistic analysis flaws all "actions" that follow on the actor's part, the means-end scheme.

But I may also want something outside the everyday world, something which lies in the transcendental world. I may want to make a poem, and despite the expression just used and despite the fact that there are, of course, aspects of making in every poem, it would be a great misunderstanding to analyze a poem predominantly from the point of view of its having been "made"; the ground of its metaphors, symbols, comparisons, images would be missed. In similar fashion, I may want to inject a new spirit into somebody or something, be it a scientific discipline, a particular individual, a style of art, a religious organization, a political government; such wanting may be indistinguishable from having a mission (with all the dangers of having a mission).

All living things have needs and may well have desires. Many animals are said to make things (nests, dams, caves, etc.). But I don't know what it would mean other than to commit an anthropomorphism, to say that in doing so they follow the means-end scheme. At any rate, to want a transcendental aim is uniquely human.

20

Again, as so often before, I didn't know how to continue, without any doubt that I would and must continue. This was so despite several days spent on rereading more than half the manuscript and leafing through the rest; nothing came of it. Then I noticed that the last entry was dated the day after something important happened to me; but obviously I didn't think of making it a part of the text. Perhaps I was too busy with my topic, "wanting," or thought it irrelevant to my enterprise, however hard I would be put to define either. Perhaps I thought what had happened had happened only to my body, which would have been contradictory to my view of the unity of body and soul. Or for a related reason: that the episode was only of private idiosyncratic but not of public interest. The topic certainly is—and I know how I must go on.

The public/private contrast is related to the transcendental/empirical contrast. The latter is the one I worked with in O Loma!, considering myself the subject in the constitution of whose self the readers were invited to participate. The distinction served above all to determine what to include and exclude from O Loma!; I would include only that which was inseparably unique and universal, and exclude all that was not; to discuss the latter I frequently called gossip. I could also have called it private or idiosyncratic but didn't, probably because I wanted to sharpen the contrast, to place the two in two different worlds. Was this on the way to the world as a stage? And what is more: was it an implicit critique of our society in which people play roles they don't understand? The public/private contrast appears in a sociological perspective, and its concrete form, that is, what is considered one or the other by whom depends on the structure of the society being discussed. The first contrast is part of the everyday world; the second, part of the transcendental world; the two pairs belong to and thus presuppose two different worlds.

What had happened to me which I excluded from these pages was that I stumbled and fell, bleeding profusely and needing several stitches. Not mentioning it here shows that I was victimized by the popular Cartesian division of body and soul, which it took my inspection of the date of the day after the accident to realize. I thus have recovered my continuity, which before had been damaged, and I have learned—including the confidence that I will know how to continue.

21

As follows: another contrast, related to public-private and transcendental-empirical is sacred-secular. This one comes out of the world of the social scientist, who here wants to account for a social institution, religion, or to construct types of societies and their change from one to the other. But "sacred" has come to have a more general use as that which is not and cannot or ought not to be discussed or is taken for granted.

From the middle of the nineteenth century (Henry Maine) to the middle of the twentieth (Howard Becker, Robert Redfield) with, around the change of the centuries, those decisive for the twentieth Ferdinand Toennies and Emile Durkheim, social scientists have tried to come to terms with industrialization by devising two types of society of which we, that is, the writer and his contemporaries, have entered the second, later one.

In slightly different words, they tried to come to terms with, or make sense of, industrialization and its concomitants—bureaucratization, urbanization, technification, etc.—and were ambiguous about it. On the one hand they longed for what they thought of as the idyllic, peaceful, simple nature of the past; on the other, they had to approve of the present and future society because that was the one they lived and made their living in. I believe that most people today know this ambiguity, perhaps even more keenly than these thinkers did. Under the impact of the disasters of the twentieth century, the conception or philosophy of (Western) history, from "sacred" to "secular" society, which found its most jubilating celebration in Auguste Comte's three stages (religious, metaphysical, scientific), seems to have receded before indifference, skepticism, uncertainty, rejection, despair. But we can also ask where we are going in the light of what I think is the single most fundamental change and potentially the final disaster: the possibility of our ending all of our lives. Here we are back to surrender-and-catch as one response to this crisis, the response being the suspension of all received notions because in their totality they have not prevented us from getting into our crisis. The catch, as always, is unpredictable, but the hope and reasonable expectation of surrender to our crisis or to aspects of it is that the catch will be pertinent on the way to solutions.

22

Thus back to the beginning. But what is beginning? The preoccupation with surrender, it seems. I just repeated, at the end of the preceding paragraph, my own answer to the question of how I must respond to the unprecedented situation of humanity (see *Survival and Sociology*), that is, to stay open to surrender and to learn and tell more about it. I believe that this writing is true to my answer. The object of its surrender was the relation between *Vorgang* and Loma, a relation in which the latter, Loma, came to be outshined by the former, *Vorgang*, the first, ground-breaking, and pathsetting case of surrender-and-catch, with Loma as an experience of surrender and its catch, among other things the naming of its kind. This is the essential relation between *Vorgang* and Loma. But how does this save humanity?

23

Obviously, surrender, let alone the relation between surrender and surrender, such as between *Vorgang* and Loma, does not save humanity. To believe that would be an incredible case of word magic (not that such word magic does not exist). The reason why surrender by itself cannot save humanity is that it concerns only what is uniquely human, only the transcendental human being. But being a mixed phenomenon, humanity must be saved by means which concern both "empirical" and "transcendental" features of human beings. In other words, they must reform society, that is, social organization or social structure and institutions. Everybody knows how difficult this is because of vested interests, as well as because of the lack of a satisfactory life aim, the most common aims, money and its power, having turned out to be felt mere means without ends.

I would feel like a fool if I tried to list particular changes that would increase humankind's chances of survival; my knowledge of economics and politics is far too poor for me to have a voice. What I claim to have some knowledge about is surrender in general and *Vorgang* and Loma in particular. This knowledge gives me the hope that we will survive, that the acknowledgment of the terrible nature of our crisis will make us, even if more nearly instinctively, crawl out of it so that we no longer will have to live as described in the harrowing scenes of *Vorgang*, not ever in the horror of totalitarianism, against which the total experience of surrender fights.

24

I did not know how to continue. In the morning I lay in bed and thought of it. I remembered sitting next to a young woman I liked very much, listening to a piece by Mozart, piano concerto no. 26, which moved me to tears; I thought I heard the creation of music itself. The memory brought tears to my eyes as the original experience had done. And made me think of "With the cloth of shame I covered my face and passed on," the end of *Vorgang*, and made me think of what, if anything, I knew of humankind, my ostensive concern—at least in the last section. I answered: nothing. I don't know what humankind is except in the irrelevant statistical sense of the sum total of all human beings. Where did I learn the words humankind or humanity? I learned them in institutions which ornated their statistical meaning with virtues of all sorts, including goodness and beauty. Thus in being ashamed and escaping I not only recognized the moral dimension of interpretation, as I came to understand in my attempt to analyze Hannah Arendt's letter, but I also—just as unwittingly—expressed a longing for surrender such as overcame me when I listened to that Mozart piece. And what does this mean? Does it mean that I can bear analyzing, interpreting, thinking, only to a certain point or for a certain time before I no longer resist the longing to let go? I fear the answer is yes. Nor do I think that the quality of either thinking or feeling diminished thereby; on the contrary, it is heightened by the affirmation of both.

I think that what I mean by humankind which surrender serves is an ideal to the approximation to which surrender and its consequences and relations contribute. This finding is the old finding of the relation between humanity and surrender, the good society and surrender. This sounds as if we were back to an earlier phase of our effort, but I think that a different interpretation is more correct, namely, that a new surrender has confirmed a previous surrender. The identity of the outcome, of the catch, of both, shows that I at least cannot go beyond but have reached the limit of my capacity to surrender. (I need not add that this may change in the future.)

25

The future exploded. Unexpectedly, very late and still prematurely: "With the cloth of shame I covered my face and passed on": I've never had the courage to take the cloth off and stop; I've kept on passing on, face covered, kept on face covered passing, on. Thus here too: not uncovering myself holding forth on the moral nature of interpretation! How ridiculous, how hypocritical—instead of confessing, face and mouth naked! But this, my fellow human beings, is as far as I can go now; I continue to hope; with the cloth of shame I cover my face.

Notes

1. First published in *Das Silberboot*, 1951, then in *Vorgang und immerwahrende Revolution* (Wiesbaden: Heymann, 1978), 75–84.

2. Developed in *The Human Condition* (Chicago: University of Chicago Press, 1958).

CHAPTER 5

To Loma

1

I am still writing about me here rather than about Loma: I am not there yet. I don't know what it takes for me to get there, but I am in no hurry. The table is still ready for the Loma materials. Again: what makes me feel I have all the time even though I am tired, weak, depressed—maybe indifferent! I can't believe I wrote this word when I am so eager (or anxious?) to write "the book on Loma," to find out what happened to me there which resulted in "surrender-and-catch" and what this implies and all *this* implies and so on *in infinitum*—implies surely not just for myself, since to surrender is to become human, that is, thrown back on oneself, which is what one shares with humanity, as I said so long ago and hold true.

I wanted to write what I just wrote, or something of the kind, even though I'd have very much liked to read all I have written here thus far; it would be the first time. Most of it I don't remember. I suppose something in the preceding pages—they began, I just checked (already!) six weeks and a day ago—makes me want to recall it now: this, too, would mean inspecting a deeper layer of the palimpsest[1] which is in the making, but it would be different from what I had in mind for "the book on Loma." The difference is that going back in these pages is going back to what you the reader, too, has been witnessing. By contrast, you, reader, do not know the Loma materials except for those which in the making of the palimpsest emerge; here, the reader is a witness, can go back to the same "materials" as I can; there it's the selecting, and the reader knows only what I tell. An act of faith is required of the reader, while here all the cards are on the table.

The way to avoid the necessity of the act of faith would be the reproduction of all the Loma materials. But in this case, the reader would have to make the book, out of this heap of papers and other documents. It seems that the act of faith is unavoidable, and the question is whether the book's author merits it. I have never forgotten the question of an unknown listener—who has since become a dear friend—to a talk of mine on surrender. He said during the discussion: "This sounds alright, but how do I know you aren't a charlatan?" To which I didn't know what to answer other than to look him in the face and say: "Look at me, look at my face!" The beginning of our friendship. Please, reader, do look too!

2

I am still eager to read all I've written here, to see what it leads to, to understand its nature, to understand where it takes me, takes us. But first I must record the problem that has emerged (whatever else these pages may teach me): how to constitute an object, indeed how to know or learn what object I wish to constitute: Loma? The book on Loma? The meaning of Loma? And then: how to lift this object out of the undifferentiated universe—the undifferentiated universe of my memory, the undifferentiated universe which my memory is. Here is the first clue to an answer: this undifferentiated universe is inseparable from myself. Of course, there is an external world; the house I see across the street looks as it did yesterday, and the weather which changes the look of the house as it itself changes is as external or objective as the house. The constitution of the object "house," my constitution of my object "house," are certainly problems, well-known problems, but my object here is not the house, it is not in the external world. Here the question is: what is my object in this writing? (Not: what am I "writing about," or eager to write, if only the object came out of the air and jumped on the stage for me to describe, perhaps even to copy.) The object is in myself, *is* myself, as much one as the other, inseparable from my relation to it. It is as much Loma, that (almost gone) very small village (located in a unconfusable point on this planet) as it is my memory of it, as the retrieval (mostly with the help of my field notes and other materials) of my memory of it, as my thinking about and assessing of an infinite number of elements in all this—thus how to articulate? I am reminded—perhaps this will help here—of what Hannah Arendt wrote (you may recall) about *Vorgang* (at least it makes for continuity—I wrote *Vorgang* in 1935, and Arendt commented on it in 1957):

Vorgang has interested me uncommonly.

The snag in the matter is that the interpretation [*Auslegung*] in principle is infinite and that this infinity-in-principle, if it cannot be in turn contained [*gebannt*] in a poetic or cognitive [*denkerische*] form, dissolves [*zerfliesst*]. . . . It is hard to understand why you don't let the interpretation be followed by the interpretation of the interpretation. And if you think about it, it is even harder to understand why you don't keep on writing at this piece, the *Vorgang*, until the end of your life. The only thing that stands against it would be life itself.

Might I not learn from this where I am now, probably in both senses of the expression: in this writing and in my life? (I mean the former but don't know whether I should.) Let me recall what happened in *Vorgang*: there was no threat by the "fundamental infinity" of interpretation because it *was* "caught in a poetic . . . form" (headed *Vertraumung*, literally "somnification," but neither the German nor the English word exists), from which or rather from the English translation of which in O *Loma*! I quoted here on February 17 (palimpsest!).

3

What happened—what Arendt refers to as the interpretation being "caught in a poetic or cognitive form"—may also be described as the "world" (in Alfred Schutz's sense) of interpretation being replaced by the world of poetry or cognition: the interpreter (I, almost sixty years ago) yields to the "need for closure," finding further interpreting unbearable, or fruitless, or boring, and, longing for a self-consummatory state of being, which interpreting was but no longer is, creates art (for instance). History (including its palimpsest character) vanishes, time vanishes, the moment is all there is.[2]

Well, isn't this, this "being caught in a form," what I am waiting for, longing for here? So that I could simply *tell* the story of Loma? There would be no problem of defining Loma: it would be there, in my words, and the listener to my tale would be in the "world" of Loma—which would continue to be inseparable from me, that is, from *my* world. Of course, the reader might also want to leave this world and look at it, from the outside, from the world of analysis, asking whatever questions may arise. The reader, then, would first be in the world of Loma (attuned to it, to use another Schutzian term[3]), moving, even singing along with it, but at another time would leave it to take a look at it from another outside, another world (that of critical attention, psychology, literary criticism, or any other of an indefinite if not infinite number of worlds).

My location here and now is very different from the reader's. I *know* there is such a world as the world of Loma, and I have at my disposal a large number of its elements (memories and documents). But I must still put them together; this is "where I am now"—and suddenly the two meanings of "where I am now" become one: this point of this book is this point in my life.

4

How does one, how do I go about "catching" the "fundamental infinity" of interpretation in a (poetic or cognitive or any) form—other than by longing for it to happen, that is, hoping for grace, for inspiration? Keep on thinking: I have —already *we* have?—reached the point to rereading all the pages leading up to it.

At 12:39 I wrote:

The tree I see through the window, the tree I have known for 34 years, is of an unbearable presence, of a recognition that leaps at me, and I must yield. But where can I go? To the tree, only to the tree, I must hold on to the tree, kiss it, if I don't want to be crushed by its enormous weight!

The earth is so heavy, the pen is so light. What hope is there for writing the "book on Loma?" What hope? The heavy tree and the light pen in the course of the book on Loma: I am writing it!

I couldn't have written this if I hadn't heard the "Spring Sonata," which as a boy I used to "play," technically quite inadequate but crazy about Beethoven, genius, as I am now, only now with unquenchable tears.

The genius of Loma!?

(Just a few words, here and there.)

(Now continuing.)

Yes, but:

I was taking a shower and found myself looking at the tiled wall of the shower stall. For some reason I found myself looking more closely, as I was getting closer to the wall (nearsighted). I focused on the inverted "T" formed by two tiles, or rather by their boundaries, the interstices between them, they are filled with grout, completely dry because the shower stall and thus the tiles and grout are probably as old as the house, some 60 years. The grout was not smooth, I could see, and I was looking at, almost contemplating, the gritty surface of the thin line, grayish, between the white tiles. I was suddenly very happy, and quite surprised! Somehow the whole world, and I don't mean—didn't feel—just its physical size (which indeed I can't imagine), had shrunk into this meeting of two lines at right angles, at the unforgettable, as it were vanishing and yet so overwhelmingly present point, not just the world in its materiality but all problems as well, all problems, personal, of poverty, injustice, corruption, waste, collective psychosis and suicide, dodoism, dadaism, all isms together, they had been absorbed by this point, suspended, neutralized in it, and I knew this! This is why I was so happy—but why was I so happy? For what I just said is really no explanation since I also knew—or perhaps I really didn't or didn't really—that no problem had gone away (or, actually, had only gone away from me . . .). I felt that which this means: I no longer feared to die. As if I had come to know something which enabled me to die. I felt serene in the face of death. I must ordinarily be very much afraid of it, partly because "I still have so much to do," figure out and tell what I find, partly because some people I love and who love me would not be serene and might not know of my serenity—and, of course, I mightn't be serene either.[4]

Earlier this month, somebody wrote me:

You don't mention Blake, but I feel how always you're hoping, and sometimes succeeding,
>   To see the world in a grain of sand,
>   And a heaven in a wild flower;
>   Hold infinity in the palm of your hand,
>   And eternity in an hour.

I knew these lines—why hadn't I thought of them when I drank in the inverted "T" in the shower stall? Of course, what both Blake and the inverted "T" are instances of is Hannah Arendt's infinity of interpretation caught in a (poetic, I suppose) form, that which, it seems, I continue to long for.

5

Right now my problem is: how do I trace all that has led to "Loma" having meant and having led to what it has led to? And what would it be worth to accomplish the task of answering this question? Who am I to put myself into the very center of the world, to ask how I have become who I am, also considering that in the shortest time I will be no more? The answer, *hypocrite lecteur, mon frere*, indeed, is that I am exemplary, my memory, my worlds are exemplary: I am a transcendental subject; my name is *human being, Jedermann, everybody*. I just remembered and shall try not to forget.

How to go about finding an answer to the question of what "Loma" has meant and led to? I know only one method that is promising: the palimpsest;

start with something today and whatever association "Loma," any phase or aspect of it may it remind you of this; it is bound to throw light on things past, including things even farther back than Loma, and what is not thus associated is bound to be, or at least to remain, irrelevant to my formation or at least to those of its components that may account for meaning and implications of Loma.

6

Several things have come up that must be and now can be taken care of: the empirical versus the transcendental subject; the question of where Loma begins; and as we'll see now, the idea of the palimpsest also including earlier writing pertinent to something emerging now.

First, on the empirical versus the transcendental subject. The empirical subject is the subject of the world of everyday life, a few of whose characteristics are listed in the telephone book and many more in a curriculum vitae or *Who's Who*. The transcendental subject is that of any other "world" by which it is absorbed, such as the world of religion, literature, philosophy, art, music, the writing of this book: what all these and other absorbing worlds have in common is that they are exclusively human.

What have I come to mean by "subject"? And where do the distinctions between the empirical and the transcendental subject as well as between the worlds of everyday life and surrender come in?

We get a first clue if we substitute "*Cogito, ergo sum*" with "*Non cogio, ergo non sum*," I don't think, therefore I am not; I am only when I think. What is the opposite of "being" ("I am"), what is my mode if I am not thinking? It is mere leading a life, mere functioning,[5] that is, following a habit or existing under any one or more varieties of compulsion. To repeat: thinking is not the only mode of being, for by "being" I mean any form of "gatheredness," absorption, any noncompulsive state of dedication to something or somebody, active or passive or mixed, for example, housecleaning, cooking, making love, painting (a wall or a picture), any self-consummatory state or activity.

The difference between the empirical and the transcendental subject is a difference between the world of everyday life with its habituality, absence of doubt about itself, taken-for-grantedness, and that world which "brackets" this one or leaves it behind for whatever other world. The transcendental subject is no longer the mixed phenomenon man is but the exclusively human, unique-universal being.

This, however, must now be qualified: I do not mean the transcendental subject to be characterized by *all* exclusively human traits—thus I already argued that the catch of surrender cannot be evil.[6] But how beyond claiming and arguing the *moral* character of surrender do I justify *excluding* exclusively human features from the idea of the transcendental subject, the unique-universal human being? How exclude murder, rape, theft, cheating, all other crimes and sins, all of which are purely human and nowhere else to be found? The answer lies in *cognitive love*, a synonym of surrender. The transcendental, unique-universal subject is possessed of those exclusively human characteristics which come into view in cognitive love.[7]

The irrelevance in love of social characteristics might suggest or indeed prove that love transcends them, makes of lovers transcendental subjects, transforms the empirical subjects they are. But we can be more accurate: it is the very unconfusable unique features of the lovers—*this* voice, *this* turn of the head, *this* curve of the mouth, *this* response—which is loved or for the sake of which the lover is loved. These unique features mean everything, make lovers cry in recollection, make them long for them—but not disembodied: make them long for them as *embodying* the lover. They represent the lover; more: they make the lover present in all presence, thereness, hereness. What then is universal about them, what makes me say that in surrender—including love—the unique and the universal coincide, and further that we cannot get at either except by way of the other? Surrender is cognitive love; it wants to recognize, to know. "Carnal knowledge": lovers want to become one also physically. Their unique features, in which they delight and over which they cry, make them experience the universal which is love.

Their social characteristics do vanish, but this they do in every full engagement, I am then fully that being which is doing these things, just as the lover is exhaustively defined as that being which is loving or making love. And—again—the murderer, swindler, liar, thief, lecher, who is also exclusively human? It took me a long time to find an answer, which I cited before and I now restate: The answer lies in cognitive love, a synonym of surrender. The transcendental, unique-universal subject is possessed of those exclusively human characteristics *which come into view in cognitive love*. That is, they come into view in surrender to the question of who the purely human, transcendental human being is. Such surrender, I believe, shows that the murderer, swindler, liar, thief, lecher are as mixed phenomena, human beings in the everyday world, but specialists in certain characteristics or activities.[8]

7

The second question that has come up is where Loma begins. But here I must interrupt for a moment to announce, to myself as much as to you, my observation: I feel that the book has taken off, has begun to move on its own, that the world of the book has become autonomous, no longer dependent, except for its means, paper and ink, on the everyday world. In continuing, I shall observe this development and whatever changes in it, if any, that may occur.

As I was writing this it became clearer and clearer that *this* is "the book on Loma," part of which the fishskin-colored mouth had told me I had done. Even though obviously—obviously now—I didn't hear all of it or remember only how part of it gave me comfort, made me feel new hope—it has the same effect now.

But now to the second question, where does Loma begin: what I mean by Loma, no matter how vaguely as yet, did not begin with my first visit. I had been in this country only a few years and was getting acquainted with American sociology.

My first extended stay, two months in the summer of 1942, was to have been devoted to teaching social science to teenagers who had come from other parts of the country to bring some income to a school founded by a Chicagoan who originally had come to be near Frieda Lawrence, D. H. Lawrence's widow, to do a study of the writer. But this man had become attracted to the place and started the school for local children, whose education he found woeful. It became clear at once that the "students" weren't interested in studying but had come to have a good time. The director of the school, who was quite eager to know more about Loma, suggested that instead of teaching I make a house-to-house survey of the community. With some help I prepared a questionnaire in Spanish and supported by the Justice of the Peace, one of the most respected members of the Spanish community—90 percent of the total population of about two hundred—I managed to get it filled out.

I had arrived in the United States only in 1939, ignorant of American sociology but eager to "learn it," encouraged and helped by a very kind professor, of the Chicago School, at Southern Methodist University where I had been lucky to find a "research assistantship." The survey of Loma gave me the opportunity to practice sociology as I had come to understand it here. I got information about ages, children, living in the house and elsewhere, incomes, land ownership and other possessions, wells owned and shared, their depth, their distances from house and outhouse, and much more. I subsequently tabled all of this, with a bit of history of Loma and a few generalizations, producing a very large number of tables, a storehouse of almost entirely uninterpreted and unanalyzed information, a caricature of "American sociology."[9]

8

In what sense was this *not* the beginning of "Loma"? In the sense that that first stay carried no foreboding of what would happen during and in consequence of the next and longest, in 1944. That stay developed six years later into, above all, the *expression* "surrender-and-catch" which I have tried to explicate, or decipher, ever since.

But here, exhilarating to say, there has occurred a beginning: I found myself, quite unexpectedly, presenting for the first time some "Loma materials." Thus the book, which is on Loma, has begun—to repeat: as a surprise.

Here then is a beginning which happened, like a conception a couple can do no more than hope for. But this is not the beginning the problem of which has come up here, namely where I begin, and on what grounds, my story of Loma or my book on Loma. What was and is problematic about this question is the fact that Loma would not have hit me, in 1944 and subsequently, in the way it has, that is, would not have led to "surrender-and-catch," if there had not been the encounter between Loma and myself: myself such as I had by then become. Thus it would seem that the beginning of the book on Loma starts with myself, with the effort to account for my having become such as to respond as I have to my 1944 stay in Loma. With my birth, then? But my birth in turn was a result, not only a beginning.

Thus, there is no ultimate beginning—just as there is no ultimate, or final, cause. But there is a difference between ultimate beginning and final cause, the difference between a "meaning chain" and a causal chain. What I want to know is the meaning of Loma, how it has developed, how it began. There are intimations of the idea of surrender-and-catch—which is certainly close to the center of the meaning of Loma, probably a clue to its beginning.

Last year I reread some very old essays I had written as a very young man.

Summer 1992

[These essays] are variations in the formulation, or in the effort to find a formulation, of my basic experience, of the basic experience of my time: the questionability, uncertainty, baselessness of everything, the terrible need for finding a ground on which to be able to stand. I quote from one variation:

[1931]

Finally [after Jaspers and Mannheim] we want to call attention [note the juvenile, bashful-megalomanic *pluralis majestatis*] to an essay which appears to offer insight and a challenge that is similar to ours: *Was ist Metaphysik?* [What Is Metaphysics?] by Martin Heidegger [Bonn, 1929] . . . this essay tells, with almost poetic immediacy, of his [Heidegger's] own life, namely, in developing the concept of "nothing," when Heidegger neither finds nor could accept a rational definition but instead reminds us of the feeling in which alone Nothing can be experienced: anxiety. Only out of this ineluctable feeling is the concept of Nothing hypostatized.[10]

And note this, from "The Poet and Sociology" [1931]:

Don't ask, what is he really talking about? You still proceed with old methods, against which I defend mine. You still think: here is the theme, "The Poet and Sociology," and now it is my task to write about it according to a reasonable scheme. But I am helpless. For what does "the" mean? What does "poet" mean? How is the relation to be understood, or is this not what "and" means at all? And what does "sociology" mean? And after this endless series of problems, where would there be a scheme? Why, all of this is problematic. No, this method is false, arbitrary—you can't do anything concrete for me against it. And this essay is this coming to terms. When you have read the essay and somebody asks you what the author talks about, then it would be wrong to answer that he first describes this, then that, etc.—no, this would be wrong; although all this is in it, as it may seem, and although one could not talk about anything. Instead: there is something: The Poet and Sociology: and there am I: and then:
More can really not be said, you understand me?[11]

Is this not the description of the catch of surrender, a surrender in which the commonsensical everyday understandings of the words in the title, "The Poet and Sociology," and the sentence part of which they make up are suspended, "bracketed"? And is what I advocate not the solution Hannah Arendt argues for to end the infinity of interpretation—the "poetic or cognitive form"? True, my quotation and Arendt's comment deal with the end of a given piece of writing (an essay, an interpretation), but the end is relative to that particular piece of writing and is also a beginning: we are dealing with a chain of meanings, a meaning chain. Its beginning also, and not only its end, *happens*, just as the "poetic or cognitive form" happens: it is made by the human being who is attuned to or guided by what is happening.

In contrast to a meaning chain, a causal chain is not composed of meanings, but of causes which gain meaning exclusively by (human) interpretation;[12] in themselves, they are unmeaning, and it is also human interest or curiosity alone that chooses the investigation of a particular cause (or effect), even though the causal chain is infinite in both the antecedent direction (every cause has a cause) and in the subsequent direction (every effect has an effect), whether human beings understand any link in the causal chain or not. (Also see chapter 4, section 15.)

We can phrase the difference between meaning chain and causal chain also in the conceptualization of Karl Manheim's distinction between intrinsic and extrinsic interpretation:

> Intrinsic interpretation relies on the interpretandum as its only source; extrinsic interpretation goes outside the interpretandum in its effort to interpret it. Causal explanation is an extrinsic interpretation; in fact, "causal explanations are not, properly speaking, interpretations, but determinations of un-meaning causal nexuses. They are concerned with the ascertainment of all those processes which, in themselves un-meaning, that is, not understandable, can merely be observed in their regulations of the context of meaning to be interpreted." Causal explanation is extrinsic to the interpretandum because it resorts to features of the cosmos (processes, laws) which, though at work in it (being "preconditions"), are foreign to it in their meaning (are not "presuppositions").[13]

Please notice that we have begun to make a beginning of "the book on Loma," that is, *the meaning of Loma*! If you don't see it yet, I trust you will.

9

I discover that (at least?) the beginning of "the book on Loma," possibly all beginning, is like the book itself, in layers, a palimpsest, with, as we realized before, no ultimate layer—no ultimate beginning, no more than a final cause or a final effect. Certainly the quotations from 1931 are not the deepest layer, but I can find no deeper ones, although it is possible that if I were to look into even earlier writings I could. Yet I have the feeling that this would add nothing to my grasp of the beginning of Loma. I am surprised by this feeling and am trying to account for it. I think its reason is that the 1931 layer identifies the direction in which Loma lies and that precedents could do no more than that either.

You may recall that after describing my 1942 house-to-house survey of Loma I said that this was not the beginning of Loma (section 7 above) because I had "no foreboding of what would happen during and in consequence of the next and longest" stay (beginning of section 8 above). Now, having discovered older layers, here has arrived the time to tell what did happen:

> following my longest and most important stay in Loma, my questions have come to be: what did it mean to study these people? What was the nature of my research, my contact with Loma? What did it mean to collect "field notes"?

What was their meaning? Who was I to have gone to Loma, what had I done there, what was I to have done? What had I inquired into? How had I gone about it, how was I to have gone about it?

In the field [these] questions only *began* to trouble, fascinate, exhilarate, and prod me; there is nothing explicit in my notes. The "field," as soon as I saw it, struck me as a landscape such as I had not known before. It was high, calm, yet exciting, with sagebrush rolling wide, rolling up the hills, mesas razed flat, shaking their green brown hues into nothingness buzzing with flowers: purple, blue, lemon tufts in the gray circled by rocky tables. The clear, blue-seamed plain receded in a constant quiver toward the glassy ranges of mountains under the darker blue sky, where shy smoke rose from earthen houses. Life here seemed different and splendid. And I was drawn to the people. The Spanish-speaking ones: the young, alive, beautiful, ugly, endangered; the old, ripe, sad, and slow; those not young, not old, drifting, confused. I was impressed by the two or three Anglo pioneers left, by their sparse looks, their generosity, by the parents of one of them who were in their nineties, by the respect of these old people and the Spanish old people, by wisdom, I thought, of those everywhere who stayed on the land.[14]

For my longest stay in Loma, in 1944, I had an agreement with the late Robert Redfield and Sol Tax, both of The University of Chicago, to develop a method by which "culture patterns" could be established so as to allow another student to go back and check point-by-point. I found this interesting, though not all-absorbing.[15] What did absorb me, even though I did not so understand it until later, were questions of the nature I mentioned at the beginning of the last quotation; what I did, at any rate, was to obey my strong need for holding on to all I could possibly keep up with.

It was years before I understood what had happened to me: I had fallen through the web of "culture patterns" and assorted conceptual meshes into the chaos of love; I was looking everywhere, famished, with a "ruthless glance."[16] Despite admonitions to be selective and form hypotheses that would tell me what to select, I was not and did not. Something I sensed was that I was not content with the probable but wanted to *know*; and I thought I might know if, instead of looking for culture patterns, for instance, I looked directly—that is, through the lens that would be fashioned by my being in Loma. "Culture pattern," indeed any conceptual scheme, had come to strike me as something learned outside Loma, something that I would import, impose, and that had been imposed on me. Instead, I was busy, even panicky at times, observing, ruminating, and recording as best I could, "everything." "Everything," I felt, was important, although the ways in which it was important would yet have to become clear. But then there also was the fear that I should be overwhelmed by the mass of my notes; I could not possibly keep in mind all the veins, lodes, and outcroppings of that growing mountain of typescript.

I came to write three versions of my "study of Loma." The big break in my preoccupation with Loma came between the first and second, for in the meantime I had found a way, which has not let me go, of talking about what had happened in the field—or more accurately, about what reflection on myself in the field showed me to have had its beginning there: "surrender." For a long time, I thought that I had "surrendered" to Loma, and my effort in the second and third versions was to accomplish two things in one: to present "surrender" and attendant ideas, and to present the study of Loma, which was entailed by the first presentation—or, rather, which *was* to be, which at all costs *had* to be, so entailed. For I finally realized after my last attempt at the enterprise that I could not possibly succeed; it dawned on me, or I marshaled the courage to admit, that I had not studied Loma with the idea of surrender in mind. The study, therefore, could not be a test of the idea of surrender; it could not be entailed by the presentation of this idea. Nevertheless, adumbrations of the idea did go back to the field, as I have tried to indicate.[17]

But now—and we are back where we were before, at the newest layer, fifty years higher than those quotations—now I had not conceptualized my surrender, had not yet found the word itself; and I think it is possible, even likely, that had I known the word and all it has come to stand for, my observations and their record in the field notes would have been different. It is in this sense only that the structure of the book on Loma in the two parts mentioned was unjustifiable.

But here, I think, is further proof that I had surrendered to Loma: the first experience of surrender in which the word occurs (six years after the 1944 stay in Loma) is a description of what also had happened to me in Loma; you see the experience before your own eyes; the words "word" surrender.

> When I drove out of the city, I was slowly becoming surprised and frightened. I felt I was no longer in streets, with their familiar smells (familiar now—by what hindsight?), but in the untouched—rocks, creeks, bushes: things unmastered, things staring me in the face, The rocks now—how glibly they were called picturesque . . . while I was shocked to realize that I knew not a thing about them and that even the [landscape] architect didn't: the rocks were merely pieces in his scheme.
>
> I, I felt, had no scheme at all; I, I wanted to *know* . . . But what? Something that had been adumbrated to me, my fear outside the city was the fear of the undefined which I had to learn to define; I had to *define* the rocks and all their fellows. I thus was in the process of surrender to the other.

I have found a quality of man: that he gains insight from antinomy, that he invents the possible because he cannot, that he gives birth despairing. He recognizes that he is alone; he understands nothing, nobody; nothing, nobody communicates with him: he speaks, and something and somebody understands him. He could not think of any possibilities were he not convinced of their impossibility.

Here is remembering and saying easily what has guided me but what all along I had not been able to say: the new, the undefined, our moment (the rock, but the moment still not come, still only shimmering in the distance). Now I can say that there is no literature that reports what happens when we see a street for the first time, when we meet a new person, see a new part of the city, enter a house not entered before, when we travel, when time, or a "point" in time, sinks us, when space, or a place, assaults us, screaming, riddle. I do not mean smells and speculations—there are noses and brains: *I mean the surrender which is the catch.*[18]

What happened to me in Loma in 1944 had happened to me—I must repeat here!—to my best recollection, three times before. I don't remember the year of the first time, but it must have been shortly before or after 1928, which was the year of the second time. I see myself clearly: walking diagonally across the snow-covered, completely white Marienplatz (Mary's Square) on the way to my violin teacher a middle-aged woman whose name I've forgotten. Suddenly it was, or I was (a wholly alien distinction), *snow*, and either simultaneously or right afterward, there was a poem, *Schnee*, which, incredibly, just happened to me, totally incredulous poet. (I wish I still had it; I remember nothing but the title, and for all I know, it was an awfully bad poem.) But this experience remained an episode, though, obviously, a memorable one. The second time, in 1928, also did, even without a poem; it happened on a walk in Garmisch, looking at the Zugspitze (Germany's highest mountain), and all I can say about it is that, like face-to-face with the snow, what I saw suddenly was *there*, inescapable, real, overwhelming. The third time was seven years later, in Camogli, 1935: *Vorgang*.

10

Finally, fifteen years after that, six after Loma in 1944, what happened on all of those occasions, including Loma, suddenly found its name, surrender and surrender-and-catch. The name was thrown at me, thrown on me, and it took some struggle before I could accept and affirm it, work with it.[19]

As I learned much later yet, after getting acquainted with Husserl and, above all, Alfred Schutz, my experiences preceding and including that of

Loma in 1944, had been "pre-predicative" (or prephenomenal), and "surrender-and-catch" was their predication—their first and lasting predication, carried further ever since.

It was in 1950, in one more experience like those mentioned (compare the quotations a few pages back), that the predication of these experiences was *surrender*, surrender on or to their respective occasions —going back in time: the drive out of the city, Loma, *Vorgang*, a walk in Garmisch, snow, and, much later, the inverted "T" in the shower stall. What, then, is the meaning of Loma? The meaning of Loma is that experience which I have come to recognize as surrender; that experience of surrender which initiated, which began, its predication. Only once I had so predicated it could I recognize the same experience on Marienplatz, in Garmisch, and in *Vorgang*, while by the time of the inverted "T" I already had the predicate at my disposal.

Thus, is the recognition of surrender on the occasion of Loma what I have been seeking, the beginning of Loma? No, now I also understand something else: that Loma has no beginning.

How so?

11

It is clear that, at least potentially, it has no end. It has had no end in me, and the potentiality refers to the fact that after I am gone somebody else may continue it. In contrast to the potentiality of endlessness, there being no beginning is a fact. I pointed out already that Loma didn't begin in 1944, with my retroactively recognized surrender to it, because I had to have been prepared for the occasion which otherwise would not have been the occasion it was, and that we therefore must go back further, beyond the preceding occasions of surrender, for even for them I had to have been prepared, and so forth *ad infinitum*.

I distinguished between meaning chains and causal chains, the former inside us, the latter outside. But did I just now, talking about my birth, not slip from meaning to cause? Certain circumstances *caused* my birth. Others caused me to develop as I did. At a certain time (say the time of *Schnee*), I had so developed that a given moment "hit" me precisely the way it did. Such a moment recurred, more than once, and finally engendered its own conceptualization —"surrender-and-catch." This was the first time an experience insisted, as it were, on meaning, gave birth to meaning, to a meaning which has continued to grow. There thus seems the cause was the basis without which meaning would not have been and would not be possible, just as there can be no spirit or soul without body. (The human being is a "mixed phenomenon.") The causal chain thus appears as the necessary condition of the meaning chain.[20] But once launched, meaning no longer depends on cause (which we realize is located in the external or objective world), but is on its own, autonomous or sovereign.

There thus is no causal analysis of meaning—but only of its occurrence and course in time: meaning is atemporal; its history is explored by social sciences; it itself, by the humanities.[21] But no meaning without its temporal (historical) home; there is no meaning that is not embodied.

Thus the claim that Loma has no beginning can and thus must now be stated more correctly. Loma understood as a meaning or meaning complex has no beginning any more than it has an end for the simple reason that it is atemporal. So are *Surrender and Catch* (1950), *Vorgang* (1935), my thought and feelings in Garmisch in 1928, and *Schnee*.

Notes

1. A written document, typically on vellum or parchment, that has been written upon several times, often with remnants of earlier, imperfectly erased writing still visible, remnants of this kind being a major source for the recovery of lost literary works of classical antiquity. [Latin *palimpsestus*, from Greek *palimpsestos*, rubbed again: *palin* "again" + *sestos* "scraped," from *Psen*, "to rub, scrap," *The American Heritage Dictionary of the English Language*, 1969. As we will see the—thus far—last form of "the book on Loma" was to be that of a palimpsest.

2. Compare kinds of sociology that make time disappear, "Sociology?" in *Survival and Sociology* (New Brunswick, N.J., and London: Transaction Publications, 1991), esp. 7.

3. In his "Making Music Together," in *Collected Papers, II* (The Hague: Nijhoff, 1964).

4. *O Loma!: Constituting a Self (1977–1984)* (Northampton, Mass.: Hermes House Press, 1989), 75–76.

5. See *Surrender and Catch: Experience and Inquiry Today* (Dordrecht and Boston: D. Reidel, 1976), index of topics under "being."

6. See "Surrender to Morality as the Morality of Surrender," in *Foundations of Morality, Human Rights, and the Human Sciences (Analecta Husserliana, XV)*, edited by Anna Teresa Tymieniecka and Calvin O. Schrag (Dordredcht, Boston, London: D. Reidel, 1983), 485–99.

7. *Transformation in the Writing: A Case of Surrender-and-Catch* (Dordrecht, Boston, and London: Kluwer Academic Publishers, 1995), 146, 14748.

8. Cf. *O Loma!*, 140–41.

9. "Authenticity in Loma and of 'Loma'" in *Transformation in the Writing* (1987), 30.

10. "Distanzierte Unumganglichkeit, Das Unumgangliche" in *Das Unumgangliche: Gedichte, Prosa, Theater, Essays*, (Darmstadt: Gesellschaft hessischer Literaturfreunde, 1988), 132.

11. "Der Dichter und die Soziologie" in *Das Unumgangliche: Gedichte, Prosa, Theater, Essays*, 119.

12. Cf. the discussion of causal and meaning chains in the preceding section.

13. *Survival and Sociology*, 105. The quotation is from Karl Manheim, "The Ideological and the Sociological Interpretation of Intellectual Phenomena" (1926), in *From Karl Manheim*, translated and edited by Kurt H. Wolff (New York: Oxford University Press, 1971), 129; second expanded edition with an introduction by Volker Meja and David Kettler (New Brunswick, N.J., and London: Transaction Publishers, 1993), 257.

14. "Surrender and Community Study: The Study of Loma" in *Surrender and Catch*, 71–72; chapter 7 by the same title in *Reflections on Community Studies*, edited by Arthur J. Vidich, Joseph Bensman, Maurice R. Stein (New York: Wiley, 1964), 233–34.

15. I formulated a tentative solution, in fact surrendering to the problem years before the term came to me, in "A Methodological Note on the Empirical Establishment of Culture Patterns" (1945) in *Trying Sociology* (New York: Wiley, 1974), 356–78. I had to find a way of keeping track of all I had observed and recorded: I described it in "The Collection and Organization of Field Materials: A Research Report" (1952) in *Trying Sociology*, 404–20.

16. Jose Ortega y Gasset, *The Revolt of the Masses* (New York: Mentor Books, 1930), 115.

17. "Surrender and Community Study" in *Surrender and Catch* (1976), 72–73; (1964), 234–36.

18. "Surrender and Catch" (1950), in *Surrender and Catch*, 9, 10, 13.

19. See *Surrender and Catch*, 20–21.

20. Cf. "Sociology and Meaning," *Philosophy and Social Criticism* 19 (1993): 287–92.

21. "From Nothing to Sociology" in *Transformation in the Writing*, 181–83.

CHAPTER 6

Loma in the Nineties—Suddenly

1

Yet, what then is Loma? It is all I remember of it, all since I was there, all that has happened and developed in relation to it since we, my late wife and I, were there in 1942—so much thinking and feeling, so much. Loma? The fancy name for a village that began to disappear with the sudden loss of its economic base more than three decades before my first visit and of which by now for some time nothing has been left but its beautiful, bewildering landscape—adjacent, as it were, to the navel of the earth. To make it present to you and I, I am thinking of the Song of Solomon, the celebration of love—the ecstasy of love. Therefore—back (back to) the beginning of O *Loma!*:

(Mon 27 D 76 toward 16)
"In these long winter afternoons." A contradiction: our watches show us they are short. But so long! Wonderfully! I am taking my walk this winter afternoon. It is very sunny, but the cold is whistling through me to my bones.

It is now that I discover this is sheer love: pure love. Rereading the Song of Solomon must have shown it to me. Well: o Loma! "Thy navel is like a round goblet which wanteth no liquor; thy belly is like a heap of wheat set about with lilies." Which is exactly the same as "How fair is thy love, my sister, my spouse!" or "I would lead thee, and bring thee into my mother's house, who would instruct me: I would cause thee to drink of spiced wine of the juice of my pomegranate." It's surrender: "cognitive love," which was lifted into a word, then into a concept, or which emerged, a whole set of ideas, all encapsulated in surrender-and-catch, but grown and growing like a tree. Here the youngest twig.

Such outburst of love, carrying cognition, explosive as it may be, is contained in the current of Loma: it doesn't even call attention to itself, the current being too vast for it. I had a first glimpse of this current when "Surrender and Catch" hit me, its writing at once surrender and catch, almost fifty years ago, but only now does its relation to Loma become clearer and more just than it was when I used to say that looking back on my stays in Loma I realized that I had surrendered to it, several years before the word had come to me, yes, in that seizure which "Surrender and Catch" is. Now I grasp the truth that there is more to it: a new life. A new approach to the world, a new understanding of everything, a place in it for Loma—but how to explicate it, and to whom? First, it would seem, to myself; once I understand it, I can tell *you*. But myself? Which is it? Self? Or other? Has the time come to "taste" these thoughts?

> What has this discussion of the other [lovers; in cattle cars to Auschwitz] to do with the other that is Loma or the other that is Australia—or the other that is me writing the book on Loma? Am I other? Is the other in me myself? Is the boundary between me, self, and me, other, blurred—blurred beyond recognition perhaps? What surprising thoughts, maybe frightening? I haven't tasted them yet. But [remember], it seems obvious to me, I am right into writing the book on Loma. (I myself? I other?)

Even my self is other, so separate from the world, for the world has dissolved into an opaque multitude of atoms which are no more than available for surrender. And "the others?"

> "What is perhaps even more characteristic of my 1984 [I wrote in "'Nineteen-Eighty-Four' and 'Surrender-and-Catch'"]—but this "1984" feels no longer tied to that or any year] is that the distinction between stranger and friend . . . both cognitive and affective, tends to dwindle. Stranger and friend disappear and are replaced by a new type: somebody selectively available, an individual suited for types of relations on types of occasions. We find a neighbor available for the exchange of garden tools, an expert of one kind or another, a lover as "sexual partner," a co-worker, a colleague, in short, one who plays a role [is a type]. . . . In being selectively available according to the occasion, all are equal—not morally equal, but shamefaced; and everybody having the same face, which is of necessity a poker face, is one of the most manifest features of people who live in a totalitarian society, a feature which also marks Orwell's *1984*.[1]

2

Am I, too, only by being selectively available? But I am shocked; how could I, how could you, have forgotten surrender, that I am, you are, in surrender, surrendering? And I, and you. We are one, I and the other are one, self and other are one, they are I. Yes, those were frightening thoughts, but I had merely lost my way, and returning to surrender has brought me back. In fact, even before this realization, there was something changed in this writing which might have shown me my false road as the dead end it is, but now I see it avoidable, that it was the urge just to write on: as if I had reached the entrance into the book on Loma, and what preceded it, these pages, were its preface to a new way of writing, the book on Loma indeed, a reconfirmation of its form of palimpsest, which is a synthesis of past writing. (I am wildly mildly astonished.) (And it would probably not have happened without Beethoven's fourth piano concerto midwife.)

3

There was a break of almost a week, and it feels that what follows is a new link in the Loma chain; thus "3." Am I still in the diary in which I wrote the pages of this section or already in the book? And how do I know, and how do you know? Remember—which I myself am weak enough to forget (from time to time?)—that I am writing to you, whoever you may be, and perhaps one day I'll find out. Are you an other, the other? I am pulling you toward me, where earlier I was both, I and the other; now I tend to be I and to experience the other as you. Does this mean I have become more myself so that I can allow the other to be you? Does it mean Loma loosening itself from me and becoming the other? How bear this if Loma is also unloosenable from me? Is what is moving me, driving me into a distance from Loma; but is it possible for Loma *not* to become an object in such a process—if this is what is taking place? Has my fantasying surrender to Loma here translated itself into what is so alien to surrender, the separation of subject and object? Or am I, not as before, self and other, but without also being other, embracing the now recognizable, identifiable other as part of myself—like my body, just like my body? Yes, I hope so.

4

"Three" so short? Yes, because I am in a quite different mood, a different mode, thus must indicate another paragraph by a new number. Whatever this means. But I'll tell you! I've just been on my stationary bike, 20 minutes, 7.8 miles. Why, even though I wanted to write, did I "have to" do the bike first? What call to duty? (Chores first, everything else afterward.) Whom would I have offended if I had sat down to write first thing in the morning (very late morning anyway)? Probably those who brought me up, but I can't name any one person who'd have told me that duty comes first. Strange that I am far more ready to suspend notions than—what; habits? Especially those that originated in duties felt?

What has all this to do with Loma? I had to get it out of the way since it has come up, preoccupying me, just as I had to get biking and much else that is morning routine, habit, duty, out of the way. And just as I had to pedal before I could write, so I have had to write this before I could return to Loma, listen back to Loma.

But even now, I haven't reached Loma yet. I was thinking of my three-times-a-week "arthritic aquatic aerobics" (a triple A). Why I am drawn to these exercises in the water, as if doing them I also had the satisfaction of doing a duty (toward my body, my health)? Yes, but I like it, too, as I like biking: in both cases, there is no problem, no question but undivided devotion to the activity, an enclave in the day, surrender to the activity, no responsibility to anything else. And then I can—with good conscience—return to what I really want to do, "the book on Loma."

But again: I was also thinking of the trip to the "health center" where I do the aerobics. A long stretch of road (several miles), then a turn right, then left (the road, still wide but now winding), not much less than a mile to the entrance road, much narrower, to the center, then into the parking area by a narrow round loop and into the "reserved" parking space, for people with an HP ("handicapped") license plate. Then out of the car and into the building, etc. The turning into the parking lot for my car reminded me of the hook at the end of a crocheting needle, as if licking itself, the road to the parking lot being the shaft of the needle. So, in this fashion, I can dream, so one can dream, even rest.

Not yet: I still must say this: it is the subject which is in the writing—it is the subject which is the writing.

5

Yes, but another subject is in the water, doing aerobics together with other subjects, all connected by a very thin web, a social web, smile-lubricated. I have no idea of any of these subjects beyond received suggestions of how to type them, and I don't know how good *they* are at typing me, perhaps some better than others; it might also be that all of them are better than I am at typing. Sociology has taken care of designating the difference(s) between the subject with which I ended yesterday's installment here and the ones I shared the pool with today by discussing types of relations and roles; but I am talking of the experience of myself writing on Loma and exercising in the water. And to find words for this is a difficult task, which needs perhaps nothing less than grace or at least inspiration, surely surrender to it, I must here let it sit, smoldering.

About this—the exercise in the water after leaving the car in the parking spot (reached by following the hook of a crochet needle)—I wanted to write already yesterday (so today I right away knew what I wanted to write about, which is very rare), and there also was another thing to which I hadn't got. This is my surprising confidence that I don't have to hurry! As if I had all the time in the world! I find the contrast between this confidence and my age strange and impressive—similar to that between my confidence in the worth of my work and my extraordinary ignorance, not only lack of knowledge, information, education, formation, but also lack of understanding, really, anything, for example, what is the transition, if this is the right word, from me in the pool doing aerobics, and me here typing? What in me changes and what does not, so that I can say "I" referring to "both"? Or: how does this typewriter "work"? Or: why is the number "1" called *one* or *un* or *eins*? Or: what does it mean to write "the book on Loma"? What is the relation between "Loma" and what I'm doing here? What is "Loma"?

6

Nonsense, the introduction is not over, I am not yet prepared, perhaps even definitively not, to write "the book on Loma." The reason I am not, not at all prepared—scream!—but on the contrary feel that I shouldn't even think of it, is what I just saw on television: Sarajevo. People alive or dead by accident unpredictably; while alive they protect themselves from freezing to death by hacking to pieces their or anybody's wooden floors, their furniture, their, or anybody's, banisters for firewood. This is humanity. But, but—but, so is Loma. This burning, to keep death from freezing away or just postpone it until the bed, the table, the floor planks have gone up in flames and nothing combustible is left, if another death, sniper death, shell death, bomb death, starvation hasn't stretched the combustibles a bit, all of this, this tiny bit, is ours, our lot, yours and mine—and so is Loma. Everywhere people, everywhere human beings, some screaming, some laughing, some murdering, some being murdered, some loving, some being loved—what am I saying?

Blabbing—squeezed by impenetrable, unapproachable pain. When I saw the television, I merely hollered and cried. The rage of the Serbians, Croatians, Muslim, and mine were one, theirs against each other, mine against the human lot and against my helplessness, no help to any of them, Serbs, Croats, Muslim, humanity, and to myself. This rage, this helplessness is one of the sources of the book on Loma, I now realize. In 1935 the nightmare of the human lot was established for me, for one of tens of millions, by Nazism, and even Nazism hasn't disappeared. "Quite different it will be and far worse." I then wrote in *Vorgang*, you may remember, "you will inhabit cliffs and stones, sharp, that your feet would hurt if you could walk, but you cannot walk." To myself nothing worse came than awful fear, but my brother and his wife would now be in their nineties if they had lived for another half century after Auschwitz. How is it possible for me to say anything at all, say anything at all—yes, yes, I know, so I felt, I said so: "in the face of the ungraspable we must be silent, but in the face of the ungraspable we must speak, speak but must be silent."[2] Thus, perhaps, the book on Loma: *Sing!* How I shall try! Perhaps I will. But already the voice has collapsed again. Collapsed in rebelling against the lot of humanity, Camus's metaphysical rebellion. And remember Dylan Thomas' great comfort:

> Rage, rage against the dying of the light,
> Do not go gentle into that good night.

Here on the high wire—on the edge.

But surrender! As I found out when I surrender to Camus's *Rebel*, metaphysical rebellion *is* surrender, surrender *is* metaphysical rebellion (and Camus's "historical rebellion" is "surrender-to" something). Just now it is dawning on me that "the book on Loma" has something to do with metaphysical rebellion: it is an act or a process of surrender, prepared for by several, even many such acts or processes, surrenders to surrender in many modes on many occasions. For the first time in the present process of surrender I have a promising hint of clarity on the nature of this book—a catch.

7

Here a new part begins; I don't know yet how to mark it; this will come. I haven't written for quite a while, probably not knowing where I was or was going. I am still not certain whether it will go on like this; if so, the only difference between its genre and the genre of *O Loma!* would be that *O Loma!* has no focus, while this one, "the book on Loma," does; the focus is what has happened to me in Loma, and what there is about "surrender-and-catch" and the surrender-and-catch that came out of it. Well, I had long thought of "the book on Loma" as a palimpsest; I believe I even talk about it in O *Loma!* and possibly elsewhere, before. I was not clear about the "genre" of "the book on Loma" but now it has turned out that these pages *are* its beginning.

A friend recently wondered whether the title of the book on Loma mightn't be quite properly *Writing Loma*. Not only a friend, but something of a genius!

It is as if I had begun to take off, still hardly above ground but rising, rising.

I suppose what I hadn't been clear about was what I would write as the top layer of the palimpsest. I thought—now I find this rather strange—that it would be external things; perhaps I remembered the beginning of the predecessor of the present adventure, in 1968, and how the deaths of Martin Luther King and Robert Kennedy made me recall a wake I witnessed in Loma, twenty-four (by now forty-nine) years before. As far as I remember, I didn't write about my thoughts on the nature of my undertaking, as I do now. But I'll find out, for the 1968 fragment is, of course, part of the "Loma material."

8

I am so slow in getting to the book on Loma. Now it's the blizzard, said to be not only the biggest of the century but of Biblical dimensions (an expression more of shudder than of measure). The world was white, and there was wind: two inches of snow the man said who shoveled it: the snowing was over for the time being but likely to resume tomorrow, perhaps worse. There were many evacuations along the coast, and most traffic stopped, airports are closed. I sat pedaling on my bicycle, it was snowing so hard, I could hardly make out the snowplow, the windows seemed marbleized with ice. (But so far my fear of electricity going out, thus no light, heat, stove, has remained empty, unlike on other occasions. Maybe technology has improved.) On my bicycle I thought of what all of this, the weather, the frosted windows, the silence for that matter that I hear *knistern* (not as loud and irregular as crackle, more articulate than rustle, although *knistern* is not always the voice of silence, which, possibly even more often, is hushing-rushing, a diminutive roar)—what all this (and infinitely more!) had to do with me-and-Loma, and *knew* the answer, but it has gone away again except that all of it, including the infinitely more, has come or is about to come or is coming together, all components in, let's now say, the enormous if not infinite flow of Loma and its tributaries, or they all are tributaries of Loma. But this is too fantastic to be true, it makes a coincidence of Loma and the world, it identifies the two—why, but they *are* the same: such, it seems or even appears, has been my experience. Which, I feel, will get clearer, I will understand better, and you will too.

I find my task very difficult. I haven't yet grasped it clearly. To grasp it clearly is part of my task. All I dispose of is hope bordering on confidence.

And why haven't I yet covered the cleared table with the Loma materials?

9

Now I believe I understand why. The table is cleared, yes, but much too tiny to hold the world. Because, yes, that's what it is about: what I had an inkling of yesterday is what Loma *is*. This is how it came: I was still in bed, not quite awake, when I suddenly realized the arbitrariness of starting "the book on Loma" or *Writing Loma* with Loma, as if Loma hadn't resulted from results of results of results, back to my birth. Thus the limit of what brought me to Loma and bore and bears on Loma is all that I can remember altogether. This is what yesterday's "enormous if not infinite flow of Loma and its tributaries" means. Thus palimpsest also of meanings, and surely there will be another layer on top of this one, and then of that one, and so forth, until the story ends, which is with my death; thus it may end at any time, but not before I die.

The "world" that Loma coincided with yesterday, the identity of Loma and the world that struck me as too fantastic to be true can be no world other than mine, and my world can be no more than the world I remember and am conscious of, a qualification I learned in bed this morning. (A twig I just observed scrapes the air. Perhaps the storm will return.)

What brought this relativization of the world about was the memory of a girl more than sixty years ago, which in turn came up because I had a letter from a man with her not-too-common last name. I thought of my love, what it was like, what it was not like, and found connections with surrender. About five years later (I am greatly surprised that it wasn't much longer), when I was no longer in Germany, I had what I retrospectively recognized was an "attack" of surrender, indeed of surrender-and-catch in one process: this was *Vorgang*. I say now that I had surrendered to my love of that girl, but not even in *Vorgang* had I conceptualized this kind of experience. And even what happened to me in Loma, nine years after *Vorgang*, took six further years for the conceptualization to explode. Thus what of *before* even sixty years ago? Sixty years ago it was love; I experienced love the first time, as far as I can remember. I was totally enchanted. I wrote a poem to her, I broke out in sweat when I saw her, I waited forever, usually in vain, for her phone call. I remember to this day—and by then I had known her already a couple of years—my trembling as I dared take her under my arm, with the excuse of crossing a street (which I see before me now)—surrender beyond this, I say now, I recognize now, was somehow too dangerous.

10

Here belongs my morning's dream, although I feel I have by now forgotten some of it. I was by a grave, my wife's grave, still it had nothing to do with her real grave. It was in a forest, in ground covered with dry brown leaves, and so was the grave, which slightly rose in the center, and on top of this central elevation rested a round tray with a tall edge, made of beautifully grained wood, light and dark brown (I now wonder if this has to do with yesterday's marbleized windows), pierced, but quite peacefully, by two soft pointed ears, very thin triangles through one of which rose a barely visible exhalation, which I knew was wonderfully fragrant, even though I couldn't smell it: it came from my wife buried underneath. And as I witnessed and wondered, I called out to her, who at that moment came through the forest toward me, and I can't recall what I said, but it expressed astonishment that she was at the same time in both places, and alive, too, in both.

She was with me in Loma, most importantly during our longest stay there in 1944 and the last time for both of us—for me at least thus far—for a few days thirty years later, when she, too, took notes (which are not yet on the cleared table).

This dream, just like the trembling arm-in-arm recorded earlier today, is intrinsic to the story of Loma, the book on Loma, *Writing Loma*.

11

I watched the television news last night, as I do every day, and was depressed by it (rather than mad, as I recently reported I had been). What any of this has to do with Loma, the reader (if any) will ask: It has as much to do with Loma, *Writing Loma*, as my soul has with my body, as the world with my body and soul. In this enterprise, nothing is separable: this fact marks my enterprise. Certainly, in the everyday world the memory of a dream would not join "ethnic cleansing" to exhaust one; in my world, the world of "the book on Loma," they (and so many more things) work together, to make me hopeless. So does the likelihood that what I just said, about the intimacy between world and self and body does not interest anybody. Thus I woke up but saw no reason for getting up or doing anything. But suddenly—I know it sounds ridiculous or unbelievable—I remembered surrender! And particularly one of its possible occasions: despair, despair of making sense, of finding any sense: "die and become"[3] because one's (received) notions are useless. Then, as I came to remind myself, one throws oneself into the situation, having regained confidence in there being meaning even if one hasn't found it yet. Maybe it is this confidence that gives me the—realistically questionable—feeling that I have time, that I must not rush or force things. I don't know whether too many blows can so rob me of such confidence that I forget it forever, lose it.

12

I wrote some of what precedes of "Loma in the Nineties—Suddenly" more than six years ago, interrupted by the necessity of meeting a deadline, but then not taking it up again until half a year ago, when I wrote most of what precedes: nothing on Loma (in contrast to the preceding section), Loma thus has evaporated, it has, as I also put it already, become a *fata morgana*, a fantasy, despite my memory of so much of it being as alive as any memory, even more than most of my memories. The reason of the difference between Loma and *Vorgang* may be the existence of a text in the latter case but not in the former, where on the contrary it has first to be written, and this is where I have got stuck. I want to give you Loma so you could be with me there but I managed only all too few snapshots most of which you and certainly I have forgotten. Thus this last section, no, this whole text even though it is about over, is a fragment. Yet for the same reason it also is a whole.

And yet and because of it, it also is the fledgling, a maggot, a butterfly, an egg, and I remember, and invite you to remember, the end of the Beginning of *Vorgang*:

My child! My child!
Let yourself be looked at, show yourself!

Notes

1. "'Nineteen-Eighty-Four' and 'Surrender-and-Catch'" in *And He Loved Big Brother*, edited by Shlomo Giora Shoham and Francis Rosenstiel (Houndmills and London: Macmillan Press, for Council of Europe, 1985), 120.

2. "Exercise in Commemoration" (1961), *Trying Sociology*, (New York: Wiley, 1974), 115.

3. *Surrender and Catch: Experience and Inquiry Today* (Dordrecht and Boston: D. Reidel, 1976), 33 (Goethe).

CHAPTER 7

Suddenly—Suddenly and Thanks to Hans Mohr

1

Paragraph. This makes me firmer in my great desire to write. But what? Or better: where, at most: what where?—I have just slept for an hour, face in hands, I had been thinking I would be sinking in the bottomlessness I felt waiting for the result of a scan before I knew that the only firm thing in the sinking was the doctor's honesty. Or it could be the more recent (what is this?) bottomlessness worded in a letter (to which I have not yet received an answer), I am still from far away. But must farther. Sleep.

2

I didn't know before I was about to type "2" that what I was going to type, whatever it might be, was a second part. After I had stopped typing I think day before yesterday I was looking, still in vain, for a sheet recording my previously unknown anxiety, sinking, sinking with any ending it, a little later, yes, recognizing as the only firm point the doctor's unconditional honesty. What I found was something I had entirely forgotten, which begins "That was a terrible dream." As of this moment, I have hardly made it out but recognize it as mine: typed on my typewriter, with my handwritten, almost illegible corrections. I haven't read it all yet, hope I'll succeed.

What hit me and makes me wonder, makes me sit up, is that I could continue whatever it is I am writing with that piece just as well as with the other one that I haven't found (yet). What does this mean? What does this mean? Is it that my mind is coming apart? Or on the contrary getting larger so as not to have to stay with any one thing any longer than it takes to get to the next? But who or what directs it, moves it where to go? It used to be interest in things, regulated by my biography. What is it now? Surely it is some searching, and if I knew what, I would name it. Do *you* know? Doesn't our smile tell that we know? But we cannot tell. An echo.

3

Two things since I wrote this, yesterday, at my wit's end (and it feels like much farther back)—two things have much relieved me, one of them much more important than the other: I think I know where that unfindable writing is (a letter in which I describe my anxiety to a friend), and I think I even know where my copy of that letter is. The other source of relief is that what I am trying to do is, "simply," to "understand" the process from one topic to another. Or what goes on as I touch my knee, lift my foot, rub my eyes. I hear of progress in understanding "such things" beginning with the consideration of the brain as a(n) immensely "advanced" computer but can't do more than remember this with hope and gratitude. In the meantime I must get that letter about my anxiety and reread it together with the page on the "terrible dream."

4

Here is the letter:

The issue is *Angst*. First, chronology. In November I had a CAT scan. About ten days earlier, the date of it had been moved back from December for which it had originally been scheduled because my oncologist—a woman doctor whom I trust wholly—had on a routine visit palpitated my abdomen and said: "You have no fat at all, so what may feel like a tumor is almost certainly your bladder. Now don't worry, I know you'll worry, but don't because I am pretty sure it's nothing, but to be extra sure let's have the CAT scan in November rather than December. But don't worry!" Within a very few days I got a phone call from the oncology department giving me the new date, which was sooner than I had expected. I don't remember any features of my mood between that phone call and the date of the scan except that it wavered wildly between feeling that I had nothing and that I had cancer and was in for another period of chemotherapy, or worse. I finally gave in, so to speak, and was taken to the hospital (by the same kindly woman who had taken me twice or even three times before and who had just turned eighty), where I had the scan, which went much faster than previous scans, but the result of which remained unknown to me. I don't recall how many times I phoned oncology but finally gave up for the day after I was told in the evening that I wouldn't hear till next morning. I phoned again shortly after 9:30 a.m., the time I had been given, but all I could do was to leave word for a doctor to call me just as soon as possible to tell me what the result was. I had to wait until ten minutes to one p.m. when my own doctor phoned, happily, that I had no cancer, that everything was fine, that she was as happy as I was.

Unless I am quite mistaken, the highpoint of *Angst* was during the night preceding the scan. I felt a helplessness such as I had never encountered in my life before. I knew this was, for lack of a better term, quite irrational because the worst that could happen was cancer or death. But that wasn't it. Instead I felt that I had no ground to stand on, that such was my life. I probably thought of many things I had produced during my life, above all writing, painting, and drawing, and of people I had loved, above all my wife, but none of these was of any avail in the bottomlessness into which I was sinking.

Later I thought of another friend, a rock climber, wondering whether he knew a similar *Angst*—and whether he hasn't done enough of it.

So long—so short!

5

And the opposite of *Angst* is triumph, such as I feel crying with Beethoven, helplessly, as helpless as I was in my *Angst*. We are both, you and I, victims of both terror and grace.

Here is what I want you to have. I wrote it the morning after the night the dream happened.

> That was a terrible dream. I probably felt sick while it went on, I certainly felt sick after waking up, if ever I have. Am I still dreaming now? I really don't know. I suddenly realized that how I was a product of my setting. I did rebel against certain features of it or the notions about them, against the understanding and practice of propriety and sweetness which means nothing, and I said nothing and was without the slightest inkling of sharing their distance from, if not contempt of, "such people," actually or suspectedly a class or more lower than we were or thought of ourselves as. I cringe at remembering how all the years I knew him I treated with contempt a classmate who I thought wasn't very bright and who lived on the wrong side of the street; in the backyard were

the stables in which his father kept his animals, his business. I'll never forget my shock on witnessing his father exploring his face while sitting sideways at his desk and swallowing what he found. And so for other classmates from "the country," with whom I didn't even try to talk about Rilke, let alone my own poetry.

And even now, 70 to 80 years later, and, what's more, after a career in social science, the absence of people I can't "talk" with is distressing. I am sure that every one of them has a story to tell but I do nothing to solicit it after a few failures.

(Afternoon.) I can no longer climb up to the height from which I saw what I wrote soon after I woke up this forenoon. I wonder what aloneness is. What does "turning-at-one" mean (with one's fellowmen, then to oneself, finally with God)? I could ask others for forgiveness, but the particular fellow I mentioned is I don't know where, if he is still alive. Much later, a colleague (who died years ago) complained to me that I continually "needled" him. I hadn't been aware of it and apologized. And I did wrong by a few women, uniquely worse by one, the one, who, ravaged by illness, finally died. I doubt that she ever forgave either me or herself.

But I feel a bit better now. Am I toward atonement?

6

I felt after writing this yesterday that I was moving toward a moral confession, that a confession was the aim and the essence of what moved me. And I did and didn't want to make a confession. I did because I wanted to unburden myself, to cleanse myself, as if admitting my wrongdoing, as if my public repentance dissolved my guilt and wiped me clean of shame. But the reader is no father confessor and would perceive my writing as an interesting or boring indiscretion, as what I called gossip (in O Loma!), whereas I meant to report on people, including myself, not as those who lived in the world of everyday life, the *Lebenswelt* but only on them as transcendental. (This was many years before the "democratization of the transcendental" and the elimination of the difference between "transcendent" and "transcendental" earlier in this book—because what I am writing now has become an additional chapter of it. See below. But I felt anything but transcendent(al) in doing wrong by others, and even using this phrase may offend discretion and taste. I wish I knew more about the great literary confessions to find out how their authors have solved this problem. As it is, however, I must abide by my feeling of inappropriateness of going on; my undescribed shame or guilt remains private.

7

But relieved as I am, where am I going? This is by no means the first time I am asking myself this question, as some of you may remember. I think the answer to the question why I don't know where I am going or where I should go is a sociohistorical answer: it is the characterization of our industrial society by "labilization." More than ten years ago, remembering my study with Karl Mannheim in the early 1930s, there

> was my concern with the idea and above all the fact of *labilization*. I have no proof, but I must have picked up the word from Mannheim, probably from a lecture since I have not come across it in his publications. As the term suggests, it refers to the disappearance or weakening of any stable order of norms, principles, guidelines, or traditions which instead have become "labile."
> [Once again]
>
> Things fall apart; the center cannot hold;
> Mere anarchy is loosed upon the world,
> The blood-dimmed tide is loosed, and everywhere
> The ceremony of innocence is drowned;
> The best lack all conviction, while the worst
> Are full of passionate intensity. [To recall from Yeats, "The Second Coming."]
>
> Labilization is a notion closely related to Mannheim's relativism; for me, it has turned out as a challenge—a challenge which, I realize by hindsight, I have tried to meet using the idea of surrender-and-catch. "I, I felt, had no scheme at all; I wanted to *know*, I wrote in "Surrender and Catch" (1950), the short piece that gave rise to all that has since followed on the topic. A very strong component of the desire to know is where we, humanity, are at this historical moment. This component has become incomparably stronger with the growth of the nuclear industry: for the first time in our history we are able to destroy ourselves and our planet—something that until a few years ago only non-human-inhuman nature was capable of.[1]

8

Since I wrote this—I see, shocked, that it was six days ago—I have tried, in vain, alas!, to find two things: First a passage of commenting on the unexpected return to writing about surrender—as here, where it went from my question where I was going to "labilization" and to surrender as a response to it, but I can't remember the route it took the time before. What I do remember is my question of what it means that, apparently or obviously, I cannot get beyond surrender. Does this mean something good or something bad?

Does it mean (good) that it survives, or thus far has survived all crises? Or does it simply prove my limitation (bad), my incapacity to suspend or bracket, to surrender to it? But isn't that what I am doing? The other problem is a different consideration of the first. It starts (and ends) with language, with the fact that we don't know the origin of words beyond historical semantics (even of onomatopoeic words) and, in addition, that we don't understand the nature of understanding. These are two abysses with which or above which we live. (Remember?) I forget who said that the ground of every true philosopher is mud or that every genuine philosopher stands in mud—I felt the sinking of anxiety; is it proper to call my surrender my muddy ground? It feels as if it made life possible; it so invites life, it encourages the jump even through abysses from abyss to abyss.

9

Am now close to typing: have already typed these words. Knew how to continue and still do, but a dream interfered, just before I woke up after having been up and having fallen asleep again, wonderfully. I didn't at first take the dream seriously, that is, didn't think that it was more than accidental, so to speak, that it was outside what I was writing, of which I knew, as I just said, how it would continue, but I couldn't get off the dream. I kept on thinking about it, I was leaning half backward, and a distinguished scholar, gray-haired, held in his trembling hands a book, and pointing to it with his trembling forefinger, showing it to me, who only could see its binding which was a Florentine-patterned flowery paper cover folded around the original binding, deceivingly similar to the one I had used to protect Alfred Schutz's *Der sinnhafte Aufbau der sozialen Welt*, but it wasn't it, and no matter how Aron Gurwitsch in his jittery hands opened it at the title page, I couldn't make it out until I finally managed to sit up and was aware of quite a number of other remarkable scholars all of whom agreed by nodding their heads that it was an extraordinary rare book, the secret source of all their inspirations, by, of course, Rabotte. I managed to make it out, not the title, but the author's name, but as Sabotte, not Rabotte, "Of course," a former know-it-all colleague corrected me, "this is the way it's pronounced, as we all know." Perhaps he even smiled, tolerantly, at my ignorance, and yet I had merely forgotten. But as soon as I had seen Gurwitsch's trembling excitement I wanted to give him, not sell him, that book—I also noticed that there was some space between the binding and the paper, either from old age or from the removal of some pages; my copy of Schutz's book compared favorably.

I did not try in any sustained fashion to make sense of this dream but knew, as I said, with increased certainty that it belonged here. It dealt with my past or one past, the past of books, scholars, words. Thus "Sabotte" reminded me of *sabot*, some sort of scandal if I remember right (I haven't looked it up in my French dictionary), and "Rabotte" got associated with *robot*, neither of which made sense to me. Nor does my frantic search for the name of the other colleague, who was or should have been in the same room as the others and whose name, I "knew," started with "P," but I couldn't find it until I looked up the authors in my dictionary of sociologists whose names started with a "P": Helmut Plessner (who had been very nice to me, but I have forgotten how).

While having breakfast I thought of the boiled egg I had taken to my apartment from breakfast yesterday and when I would eat it. (It was in the refrigerator.) I expect an old friend this afternoon, a retired lady professor, who would tell me that she had recently read an article which warned the readers not to keep eggs, once they have been boiled, in the refrigerator more than two or three hours because some, though by no means all, have been known to lay eggs in their yolk which she didn't remember after how long would result in those venomous chicks; being picked at by one of them would cause instant though indescribably painful death. Of course, she didn't know, but if she were me she would throw the egg I had away, preferably smashed and buried. But she also smiled and returned to literature as the topic of our discussion. At any rate I'd better eat my egg before it might develop terribly venomous chicks.

10

As I said I don't know the meanings of the dream or of the breakfast phantasy. But I have a sense of liberation because, I think, I have just typed more than two pages in about an hour; furthermore, they are pages that belong here (as does the dream about Mamma Packet).

And even though I continue to know how to continue, there is another short thing which (merely) postpones the continuation, another breakfast phantasy, though much closer to being acted on: I looked out of the window and saw trees moved by winds. What about, I thought, recording different kinds (species, ages, sizes) of trees in different locations (altitude, angle to surface of the ground) at different times of day and season and temperatures by different kinds of winds (from none to breeze to storm to tornado)? I am sure I cannot think, do not know, of all the uses to which the results of such a study could be put, but I am sure it would be "fun," and I thought of my humor.

What does it mean to find such a study also a joke? Does it take the sting out of death? Does it make the world a stage?

11

The world as a stage I saw the first time only a couple of years ago sitting at a small round table on the sidewalk (you may recall) leisurely sipping my espresso while watching the people passing, how they moved, what they showed and hid of themselves. I so enjoyed myself—but why? Perhaps I was so passive and approved of my passivity; my relation to the world was purely aesthetic; I must have had a taste of freedom. Of course (?), I also found everything I saw funny: the people I was watching were playing roles they didn't know they were playing, but the whole play was as far from a tragedy as a comedy can be. I embraced everything and everybody I saw with the humor of love, which was my happiness.

I remember exactly the place where this happened, twice thus far, but I am sure it will happen again whenever the weather permits it. But for this season it's much too cold. Until spring, memory alone must do. An indoor place is too crowded and noisy. But I felt depressed and I felt unruly, and tired. Suddenly, I don't know at which point of my waving, I felt relief because I had a clear question: I had to face death. At once it wasn't facing death; to put it that way was to speak as the victim of easy inaccuracy, and here if anywhere at all, I must try my utmost to be accurate.

12

But, strange, it's another day. I feel no longer confronting death or encountering death, I feel better but so weak. It's afternoon, and I am less weak than I was, otherwise I wouldn't be typing but stretched on my bed or between my arms on my desk. I don't know "what" I have; I try to describe it as I feel it and do, of course, a bad job, because it has no name to which I could refer you and you could refer me and we both would add "you know what I mean," which of course is not true, but we've got to jump the abyss. This, of course, applies to whatever we can possibly say, thus also to my effort to describe how I feel or felt.

I was all one in my encounter with death yesterday; today instead I felt my body and my soul going separate ways: I felt my usual contentment but weak enough to do nothing at all. Not to "be at one" felt bad, but since I had no pain I indulged my longing for rest. It feels, I feel, that this was the right thing to do.

It's, incredibly, a space of darkness away.

13

When I went to bed here yesterday I knew so well how to continue: rereading the last few pages, and would learn how to. But not so! Suddenly, during my couch rest, I remembered keenly how unconcerned I was about meaning, about the meanings words might have or might not have if what? If they only surprised! How unconcernedly, innocently, I was an abyss jumper! I remember a sonnet cycle, "The Fetus Kicks," which accompanied as it were my wife's pregnancy and in which in many of the sonnets the only scaffold was the sonnet form. But such unconcern goes back much further, into my late teens and is in German. I want to give an example:

> Ja, ja, die Gehirnzellen . . .
> Ja, ja, die Gehirnzellen
> Wie weiche Zigaretten schmeckt das auf dem Mund!
> Ich kann nichts weiter als in violetten Schatten
> Des Bribrabrubrabrums
> O Grinderschorf unter dem Strohhut
> Heil Abendsonne!
> Heil dir!
> Gerettet! Gerettet!
> AMEN!!!
> Terrasse Chirico Pandektenlöwen
> Schon ganz fantastisch ist doch dieser Dichter
> O komm o komm! (lies: okommokomm!)
> Ein Abendlüftchen tut mir not!
> Holst du den Tod mal eben vom Gefach dort runter!
> Grunende Läppchen um die Urfasszehe![2]

Now I am thinking of translating this and find it a ridiculous, hilarious, puzzling task—beyond the abysmal jump from language to language. Because of this language. Most obviously in the case of no or invented words, such as "Bribrabrubrabrums": a spur-of-the moment expression; it must remain untranslated. With the rest, we'll see as we try and, I hope, move along.

> O yes, the brain cells
> Like soft cigarettes does this taste on the mouth!
> I can no more than in the violet shadow
> Of the Bribrabrubrabrum
> O scabby scurf under the strawhat
> Hail evening sun!
> Hail to you!
> Saved! O saved!!

> AMEN!!!
> Terrace, Chirico pandect lions
> Really fantastic is this poet
> O come o come! [read: ocommocomm!]
> An evening breeze is what I need!
> O will you just take death down from the shelf up there!
> Greening small flaps around the archgrabtoe!

This went more easily than I expected; the praxis of translation must have outdone the theoretical impossibility of translating. In fact, I find it tempting to think of arranging a play for what has meanwhile developed into incipient characters of this poem which I wrote sixty-nine years ago: the Archgrabtoe seizing Death by the neck, while the Evening Sun shines on a painting by Chirico on the Terrace, Lions growing irritated by the Pandects' lack of flavor. Etc. The refreshing humor may yet save us from insanity of not making the abysmal leap but sinking sinking forever—whatever forever may be.

I suppose I worked in translating also with the untranslatable aspects of the two languages, their auras, to apply Walter Benjamin's term here. But who can describe what happens as we say "the same thing" in two different languages? For sure, not only the text changes, we do too.

With the help of a friend who sees better than I do I found *The Fetus Kicks* and seem to discern a shift in the meaning of the abysmal jump—from the analysis of words and of their connection to the abyss of the whole poem, with its more or less elaborate sonnet structure the irony of a satisfactory order. An extreme example:

> Anticipation of Birth
>
> Out of the pink a rising blue is falling
> and meadows give their hefty green consent:
> Far-darkling heaven's falling sepia gushes,
> consent of clouds and forest seams,
> Out of the kisses thundersticks are calling
> and waves are bent on brownish lust of waves,
> The roses wallow in the thorns' recalling
> and misty birds are bent on tricks
>
> No time for gall no time for peak and tent
> But place for falling and for high consent
> and good to be content in glorious calling
> No heart is rent no brain is vainly calling
> why we are sent is nobody's recalling
> and our appalling is our high consent.[3]

This was the first sonnet of many to accompany, as I said, my wife's pregnancy. If this is remembered, it may be possible to sense a high tension between the horror of something going wrong and the glory that the miracle of birth will actually occur. Maybe this will help attenuate the irritation of the exaggerated reliance on rhyming, especially the overuse of "calling" and variations, and make space for some empathy with an expectant father practicing his poetry.

14

Bad: five days later. However could I have fallen into the examination of poetry while she kept on taking up again and again crying, and I kept up and taking on again and again wiping the coffee grains up the tiled stove, the coffee I had poured into a funnel with nothing to collect it. "I am just trying to wipe this up," I cried into her weeping, feeling I was doing my irrelevant and useless duty, still apparently content with my progress, meantime with a big wipe realizing that it was a long time that she had died; I am referring, of course, to my unnameable wife. Whose cry and crying were so youthful, as she was altogether, a young woman inconsolably crying. I woke up as ignorant or what to do as before.

There is behind this all, I must say it now, the problem posed by this uncanny phrase from 1950: "*I mean the surrender which is the catch.*"[4] But from about the same time on I kept insisting that the idea of surrender-and-catch was a Western idea in the sense that what mattered was the catch, not surrender (see chapter 4, section 5), what mattered was what to do with the fish in the net, not get lost in contemplating its beauty, not go native but come back and report to one's fellowmen or at least to our consociates, doing what surrender asked one to do.

What has led me back to that wholly forgotten phrase "surrender which is the catch" are some lines in a letter from my friend Hans Mohr (January 21, 2000) about what I had thought of as my book A *Whole, A Fragment*:

> It [this book] is indeed an act of Surrender which is . . . the Catch that keeps changing all the time. In fact I feel now, after having read A *Whole*, that Surrender is only complete when one is able to escape the notion of Catch, when there is no longer a need for it. And so, it appears to me, in writing this work, you are open to and drawn into myriads of mini-surrenders to the moment in which you write.

Now I am more confused than I like to admit. The question now suddenly is: what *is* the relation between surrender and catch? I have always thought that I had thought it was between experience and its consequence, whatever the consequence might be. But now I rediscover the phrase "surrender which is the catch," which shows me that I knew better than I knew (if I may say so). There was in the history of my preoccupation with surrender-and-catch a slight nudge toward making one of the two: the hyphenation of the expression, suggested by Richard M. Zaner in "The Disciplining of Reason's Cunning: Kurt Wolff's *Surrender and Catch*."[5]

15

It must have been about a week ago that I left this typewriter, shot through with questions which made me lie flat. What do I think is the relation between surrender and catch, what is surrender, what is catch? Can't I get rid of my Western bias, my pragmatism? And how must I change *A Whole, A Fragment* given this new, this old problem? Do I have to rewrite all explicit statements about surrender-and-catch—or do I "simply" add what I wrote since I "finished" the book?

I answered the last question first, or it was answered, answered itself first: I change nothing in the book because it became as it did, but add these last pages because they too came or became as they did and where they did (with Hans Mohr, I'll never forget, midwife). I don't know yet how they will be titled except "7" (I'll think about "Farewell" later, it might or might not need changing); now I must get to the questions concerning the nature of surrender and catch and their relations—just noting that I used the same terminology as with regard to *Vorgang* and *O Loma!*

16

Vorgang certainly was (and is) both surrender and catch, at the same time both (and I said this and presented it as a matter of course). But what about my other experiences of surrender (of surrender-and-catch)? On my walk in Garmisch the Zugspitze suddenly overwhelmed me, and that and its unforgettableness were the inseparable catch of my surrender. Then *Schnee*: here writing of the poem, the poem itself, was the inseparable part of the experience of surrender. In the case of the inverted "T" in the shower stall, the experience was immediately followed by thoughts concerning, above all, death which are, again, inseparable from it. And what about the world as a stage and similar experiences reported in this book? I think in all cases of surrender the catch is inseparable, although it is impossible to predict when—when, before the experiencer's death and even later, by others, it will be exhausted. Thus the catch is from instantaneous to infinite.

But despite all of this, it is different from surrender itself. Surrender itself is complete absorption; the catch, irrespective of its time of occurrence, brings with it a certain distance from itself, whatever it may be. I can read, I can remember *Vorgang* or *Schnee* (if it were ever found) or the report on the inverted "T": I thus can refresh my memory of these catches, whereas of their surrenders I can remember only the comparably unspecified absorption, excitement, full and even overflowing life. And the same difference between surrender and catch is even far more evident if the catch is not a literary product but something in the world of everyday, for example, a change of occupation, friend, spouse, residence, interest.

17

But there remains that phrase, "the surrender which is the catch." But if what I just said is true, there can be or there is no surrender without catch. Still, there is a difference between surrender and catch and "surrender which is the catch." What is this difference?

Since I wrote this, several hours ago, I have done nothing but listening for phone calls which didn't come and playing with "surrender which is the catch," but above all, closing my eyes and resting, probably nodding off in between. I finally gave up "surrender which is the catch" and rediscovered, yes, rediscovered, surrender. I must surrender to "surrender which is the catch." But I don't remember how to do it. But I do remember "possible because impossible." I find it impossible so it is possible. The surrender, which is the catch. The surrender itself, which is the catch. The fulfillment, the satisfaction of surrender, which is the catch. What this means to me or for me will or will not become clear later, and nobody knows when (if ever). If it does it will be the catch at a further remove. I feel I said all, meaning all I can say on this question.

18

But there remains what from the socio-historical-political point of view, from the point of view of the everyday world, is the most important aspect of this change and this assessment of the catch: its de-Westernization. Those who think of surrender-and-catch as one can communicate as they could not when the catch was foremost in their mind—communicate with others who live lives guided by their transcendent(al) nature. What remains Western is that surrender-and-catch (remember the democratization of the transcendent[al] and the elimination of the distinction between "transcendent" and "transcendental") serves the improvement of the everyday world, while other similar religions and philosophies try to escape and replace or compensate for the everyday world—and above all, to do right by the "mixed phenomenon," body and soul, all human beings are: democracy. Every feature of such a glorious prospect remains to be worked out—a glorious prospect for a better humankind to which surrender-and-catch can contribute paving the way!

19

Farewell

Farewell, then, farewell myself, farewell you, farewell, *Vorgang* and Loma; with you, Loma, the farewell is especially moving because, as I said, I have nothing to show but abortions, which amount to a fragment. As is this whole short, heavy book. As am I, my life.

What is a fragment? A fragment is something broken off—from life; at least it is that. But why have my attempts at writing on Loma not succeeded? I think because they are not the ends I had thought I was seeking, first the community study, then cultural patterns, eventually "the book on Loma": they rather turned out to be way stations toward what I just finished. What is this? What does it mean to call it a fragment of my life? It means quite simply that it is a fragment of my life, and I cannot think of anything more to say beyond, once again, all farewell!

Newton, Massachusetts
Thanksgiving, 1999; 20 March 2000

Notes

1. "Karl Mannheim" (1988), in *Survival and Sociology* (New Brunswick, N.J., and London: Transaction Publications, 1991), 70–71
2. 1931. From *Vorgang und immerwahrenda Revolution, Prosa, Szenen* (Wiesbaden: Heymann, 1978), 72.
3. *Experiment: A Quarterly of New Poetry* 3, no. 1 (spring 1947): 188–89.
4. "Surrender and Catch" in *Surrender and Catch: Experience and Inquiry Today* (Dordrecht and Boston: D. Reidel, 1976), 13.
5. *Human Studies* 4, no. 4 (October–December 1981): 365–89.

Acknowledgments

I want to thank, more than I can say, Gary Backhaus for his numerous acts of help accompanying the publication of both *A Whole, A Fragment* and *What It Contains*. He knew the right publisher and wrote him a long appraisal of my work, which persuaded him publish it. Gary's encouragement has been invaluable, as has been his moral assistance. Thank you again and again, dear Gary!

Index

absolute point zero, 50, 52
absorption, 115
abyss(es), 36, 108, 112; abysmal jump, 111, 112; abyss between generations, 53; abyss jumper, 111; abyss of language, 47, 52; jump the abyss, 110; little abysses, 38; the two abysses, 108; unfathomable abyss of language, 44
aesthete, 35
aesthetics, 35; aesthetic critique, 11
Agee, James, 54
Angst, 104, 105
antinomy, unresolvable, 50
Antonia, 64
anxiety, 16, 21, 22, 23, 67, 68, 84, 103, 104, 108; anxiety provoking, 15; fundamental, 67
anxious 21, 23, 75
anxiousness, 22, 23, 67; question of anxiousness, 67
Apollo, 6, 30, 31
Arendt, Hannah, ix, xi, 43, 44, 46, 47, 76, 77, 84; Hannah Arendt's letter, 1, 3, 47, 52, 74; Hanna Arendt's suggestion of interpreted and interpretation, 3; Hanna Arendt's terms, 70
art, encountering, 4
Augustine, St., 46
Auschwitz, 44
autobiography, ix; autobiography, intellectual, xi; my biography, 104

Becker, Howard, 72
Beethoven, 78, 95, 105
beginning [*Anfang*], 34, 41, 43, 57, 72, 102; poetic, 12
being, 19, 22; anxious-making being, 23; being of the scientist, 18; being that is becoming, 23; being transformed into words, 23; creation of being, 20; exact meaning of being, 22; hierarchy of being, 17; higher level of being, xi; ineluctability of being, 7; meaning of being, 23; meaning of my being, 19; my being, 20; my situation for being, 17; necessary accompaniment of being, 19; our being, xi; positions of being,

12; possibilities of my being, 20; pure being, 21; show its being, 17; transformation of being into meaning, 20; translation of being into meaning, 15
Benjamin, Walter, 112
birth, 18, 19, 23, 25, 28, 37; anxiety of giving birth, 9; births of drunkenness, 17; certainty of birth, 23; giving birth, 5, 18; ineluctable birth, 37; image of the birth, 5, 23; miracle of birth, 113; my birth into, 18; at the rest moment of birth, 18
Blake, William, 79
bourgeois, 65, 66
the bottomlessness, 103, 105
Brahms, Johannes, 66
Breughel, Pieter, 49
Broch, Hermann, ix, xi, 41, 47, 49–53; Hermann Broch's commentary on *Vorgang*, 3
bureaucratization, 62, 72
"by three rooms," 4, 10, 45; "by hardly three rooms," 9, 45; "hardly three rooms," 10

Camogli, 21, 59, 88
Camus, Albert, 98
Carla, 64
Carrara, 8
Cartesian division, 71
catch [*Fangen*], 34, 44, 46, 58, 60, 69, 72, 73, 74, 88, 98, 113–115; area and means of the catch, 34; catch of surrender, 44, 81, 84; intrinsic and inextricable parts of the catch, 44
Cecilia, 64
certainty, 21; certain, 22, 23
chain: causal, 84, 89, 90; meaning, 84, 89, 90; of meanings, 84
chasm between generations, 49

Chicago School, 82, 86
Chirico, Giorgio de, 112
Clara, 59
clarity, unfathomable, 24
cognition, process of, 48
cognitive love, ix, 81, 93
Comte, Auguste, 72
concept(s), 20, 22, 23, 26, 48
conceptualization, 4, 89, 100
connections, causal and cognitive, 66
consciousness of doing, 7
contrast: public/private, 71; sacred/secular, 71; transcendental/empirical, 71
crab, 5, 15–16; crab- and snaildom, 5, 15; crab feeling, 5, 16; crabbling, 15; crabman, 16; "fear of crabdom," 16
critique, aesthetic, 11
culture patterns, 86, 116

Dali, Salvador, 49, 51
Darmstadt, 58
death, 28; confronting death, 110; encountering death, 110; face death, 110; sting out of death, 110
definition, 9
dialectic, Hegelian, 51
difference between: the empirical and the transcendental subject, 80; history and story or fable, 66; Loma and *Vorgang*, 102; "meaning chain" and "causal chain," 83, 85; the processual and the ineluctable, 26; ultimate beginning and final cause, 83; the world of everyday life . . . and that world which "brackets" this one, 80
Dionysus, 6, 31; Dionysius and Apollo, 30
dissolves [*zerfliesst*], 43, 44
distinction between: empirical and the transcendental subject, 80; interpretation and moral judgment,

46; intrinsic and extrinsic interpretation, 85; ultimate beginning and final cause, 83; wording and thought, 30; worlds of everyday life and surrender, 80
dream(s), x, 26, 30, 31, 40, 99, 107, 109; hope-dream skin, 39
drunkenness, 4, 5, 8, 9, 10, 11, 12, 14, 15, 26, 28–31, 36, 45; apartment of, 10; births of drunkenness, 17; of bliss, 37; capacity for, 15; deadly drunkenness of life, 25; desire to grasp the drunkenness, 10; drunken primordial sensation, and discharge of semen, 51; drunkenness of being ready and certain, 24; drunkenness-primordial-sensation-discharge-of-semen, 49; figures of drunkenness, 24; foaming-out of the drunkenness, 11; of happiness, 23, 25; of life, 25; lust of, 10; new drunkenness, 24; old miraculous drunkenness, 24; poet's drunkenness, 18; of power, 37; sickness and death as drunkenness, 7
Durkheim, Emile, 72

Eastern, 58, 59
ecstasy, 7, 25; ecstasy of love, 93
emotion, moral-aesthetic, 10
enchanted, 10
enchantment: deepest, 33; dispensers of, 24
Enlightenment view of knowledge, ix
ethics, 35
Europe, 54
everyday world, 58, 70, 81; everyday life, language of, 51; everyday life, world of, 47, 69, 80; improvement of, 115
existentialism, ix, xi, 48, 50; existential perspective, x; existential writers, x; existentialist attitude, 48, 50; existentialist enterprise, 48; existentialist twist, xi
explanation, 9; causal explanation, 85; explaining, poetic or scientific, 13
exploitation, 9

face to face, 4, 5, 21, 45, 88; "face to face," 9; "face to face with me," 10, 64
field, 86; fields, as yet explored, 9; fieldwork, conception of, x; fieldwork in the life-world, ix; "figure," twofold sense of the word, 68
foam, 44, 58
form(s), poetic or cognitive, 43–46, 77, 78, 84
fragment, 116; fragment of my life, 116
fructified, 36; fructifier, 6, 36

Gadamer, xi
Garmisch, 114; walk in, 88
gatheredness, 80
Gdansk, 8
Genoa, 58
Germany, 61, 99; Nazi, 6, 61
Gershwin, George, 45
Gurwitsch, Aron, 108

Heidegger, Martin, 83
helplessness, 105; helpless, 16; helplessly, 105
Hofmannsthal, Hugo von, 33
Holland, Nazi-infected, 53
Husserl, xi, 54, 88

ignorance, overwhelming general, 68
image(s) 11, 26, 29, 32–34, 36, 46, 53; blessing image, 25; image for the ineluctable, 37; imageless, 29; imageless time, 37; imagelessly, 29; images of our condition, 36; of science, 30; strong blind, 5; the time images, 37

industrialization, 72
ineluctable [*Unumgänglich*], xi, 25–33, 35, 36, 38, 40; an image for the ineluctable, 37; ineluctability of being, 37; ineluctability of the recipient, 28; ineluctable green, 33; ineluctable sea, 33; ineluctable of the writing, 26; ineluctable-processual, 27, 35; ineluctable-processual synthesis, 31; ineluctably, 30; ineluctably processual, 29, 30, 34; new ineluctable, 38
infinity-in-principle, 43, 77
intentionality, 28
interaction, 63
interpretation(s), 7, 8, 9, 12, 14, 15, 18, 23, 30, 31, 43, 45, 46, 51, 58, 60, 63, 77; endless interpretation, 58; fundamental infinity of, 77, 78; Hanna Arendt's infinity of interpretation, 79; Hanna Arendt's "in principle unendable" interpretation, 51; "in principle unendable" interpretation, 46; infinity of interpretation, 78, 84; interpretation of interpretation, 43; intrinsic interpretation, 85; moral character of, 46; moral dimension of, 46, 52, 74; moral nature of, 74; unendable interpretation, 44; unfinishability of, 65; "world" of interpretation, 58
inverted "T," 78, 89, 114, 115
investigation, literary-aesthetic, 12
Italy, Nazi-run, 53

Jasper, Karl, 83
"Jewish secret," 63
Joyce, 41, 50

Kant, 8, 34, 35, 68; Kantian appearance, 13; Kantian question, 33

Kennedy, Robert, 99
King, Martin Luther, 99
knistern, 99

labilization, 107; labile, 107
landlessness, 38
landscape(s), 7, 22, 28, 37, 41; beauty of the landscape, 61
language, 44, 45, 47, 48, 50–52
the law of yesterday, 22
Lawrence, D. H., 82
Lawrence, Frieda, 82
Lebenswelt, 59, 106
life-world, field work in the, ix
locatedness, ix
logic, 10, 37
Loma, x, 1, 2, 4, 60, 61, 62, 65, 66, 72, 73, 79, 81, 86–88, 93, 95, 96, 102; beginning of Loma, 85; "the book on" Loma, 75, 76, 78, 82, 83, 85, 87, 94–97, 99, 101; falling in love with Loma, 66; genius of Loma, 78; idea of Loma, 87; implications of Loma, 80; infinite flow of, 99; Loma material(s), 75, 76, 83, 99, 100; longest stay in Loma, 86; meaning of Loma, 60, 83, 85; myself-in-Loma, 60; preoccupation with Loma, 87; story of Loma, 77; study of Loma, 60, 87, 101; surrendered to Loma, 87; survey of Loma, 82; tributaries of Loma, 99; work on Loma, x; "world of Loma," 77, 78
love, xi, 41, 60; outburst of, 94; pure, 93; sheer, 93
lust, 10, 25, 45

Maine, Henry, 72
Mamma Pacchetto, 64, 65
Mamma Packet, 109
Mannheim, Karl, 83, 107
Marienplatz, 88, 89

maya, 58
meaning(s), 5, 12, 14, 15, 17, 19, 20, 22, 23, 33, 45, 58, 63, 11; core of the meaning, 50; clarification of the meaning, 11; incontestability of meaning, 17; meaning of my being, 19, 22; meaning of the dream, 109; meaning-loaded word, 22; not-yet-meaning, 17; of our sentences, 18; order of meanings, 18; pregnant with meaning, 14; scientist orders meanings, 17; unending and unendable search for meaning, 62; is what being is to me, 20; what-does-it-mean, 15
Mediterranean, 9, 59, 66
Merleau-Ponty, Maurice, xi
mixed phenomenon, 62, 73, 80, 81
Mohr, Hans, 113, 114
moral confession, 106
Mozart, Wolfgang Amadeus, 73, 74
Musil, 32, 41

names: naming, everyday history of, 63; "real name," 63
Nazism, 1, 62, 98; Nazis, 54
Nietzsche, 41
Novalis, 68

objectivity, 3; appearance of objectivity, 3
openness, ix; extraordinary openness to being, x
order between being and concept, 23
Organda, 61
Orwell, George, 94

palimpsest, x, 75, 77, 79, 80, 85, 95, 99
Pan and the Fairies, 6, 24
paradox of socialization, 4
paramount reality, 51, 58, 59, 69
Pareto, Vilfredo, 70

Parsons, Talcott, 70
Patricia, old, 61, 65
phenomenology, ix, x, xi
philistine, 65
Plato, xi, 8
Plessner, Helmut, 109
poem: *n*-dimensional poetry, 48; poet, 17; poetic, importance of, 12; poetry, lyrical, 48, 49; rational, xi, 48, 50, 51
pragmatism, 114
pre-predicative, 89
process, 60
processual [*Vorgänglich*], 25, 26, 29–33, 34, 35, 36; becoming of the processual, 29; processual designation, 36; processual mask, 37; processual question, 36; processual of the writing, 26; processual-ineluctable, 31

the "R," 10; "the purity of the R sound," 10; the smoothness of the "R," 4, 10, 45
Rabotte, 109
Ravel, Maurice, 45
Rebellion: metaphysical, 98; historical, 98
Redfield, Robert, 72
Red River, 61
relation between: being and meaning, 18; concept and experience, 3–4; humanity and surrender, 74; language and sense impressions, 50; "Loma" and what I'm doing, 97; something vaguely in mind . . . and the expression, 11–12; subject and object, xi, 48, 50; surrender and catch, 113; *Vorgang* and Loma, 62, 72, 73
relations, xiii
Rilke, 106

Sarajevo, 97
Sartre, Jean Paul, x, xi
scheme, means-end, 69, 70
Schnee, 89, 90, 105, 114
Schutz, Alfred, 67, 70, 88, 108
sea, 4, 10, 11, 13, 15, 17, 18, 19, 21, 24, 33, 38, 45; above the sauntering sea, 6; above the sea, 4; analogy of the sea, 13; clarity of the sea, 11; "description of the sea," 13; "face to face to the sea," 9, 45; "feeling of the sea," 13; fructifying sea conqueror, 36; glide into the sea, 6; in spite of sea, 38; "into the sea, above the sea," 10; picture of the sea, 13; rock-sprayed sea, 4, 18; sauntering sea, 24; the sea is blueing, 6; sea of death, 21, 27; "the sea is green," 33, 36; sea of roses, 21, 27; sea-benumber, 6, 36; seeing into the sea, 4, 45
seeing, empathic, 11
self-construction, x, xi
semantics, historical, 63
sense impression(s), 48, 51
senselessness, feelings of, 34
shame of cloth, x, 41, 46, 47, 54, 74
"shift," 59; shift from Loma to *Vorgang*, 4, 18
shudder, 15; full of shudder, 18; of humanity's future, 46; phallic primordial, 41; shudders of sickness and death, 7
significance, 12; importance of, 12
Simmel, Georg, 4
situation of all being, 8
snake(s), 38, 39
social science(s), 3, 59, 82, 89, 90
socialization, 4; interference of, 4; processes of, 63
society, 73; good society, 74; industrial society, 107; "sacred" to "secular," 72

sociology, American, 82; caricature of, 82
sociology of knolwedge, x, 41
somnification (*Vertraumung*), 77
split of unsayability, 16
subject, empirical versus transcendental, 80; transcendental, 79
surrealism, 49
surrender, 44, 46, 58, 60, 69, 73, 75, 80, 87, 88, 93, 95, 96, 113–115; capacity to surrender, 74; characteristics of surrender, 1; Eastern version of, 59; first experience of, 87; limit set on surrender, 52; occasion of surrender, 47; process of surrender, 87, 98; relative absoluteness of, 52; satisfaction of surrender, 115; surrender on the occasion of Loma, 89; surrender to our crisis, 72; test of surrender, 46
surrender and catch, ix, 2, 45, 54, 58–60, 72, 73, 75, 83, 88, 89, 94, 99, 107, 114–116; guilt and the political-historical place of, 55; historical importance of the idea of surrender and catch, 62; idea of, 107
surrender-to, 98; surrender to it, 108
suspend received notions, 68; of the distinction between interpretation and moral judgment, 46; suspend notions, 96; suspended, 84; suspension of prior beliefs and assumptions, ix; suspension of received notions, 47, 72
Suzuki, 54
swerve, 10, 45;
swerving, 10, 33–35; unswervable, 40
symbols, primordial, 49
synthesis, ineluctable-processual, 31–34
synthetic judgment, 34, 35

taken-for-grantedness, 80
Tax, Sol, 86
technification, 72

theory, 5, 17
Thomas, Dylan, 98
thrown back on oneself, 75
title of this book, xiii
Toennies, Ferdinand, 72
totalitarianism, 62, 73; incipient, 61
transcendence, 34, 47; Transcendence, 35
transcendent, 115
transcendent(al), 69, 73, 106, 115; elimination of the difference between "transcendent" and "transcendental," 106, 115
transcendental, 115; democratization of the transcendental, 106, 115; transcendental aim, 70; transcendental subject, 79–81
transformation(s), 16, 29, 40; ineluctable transformation, 40; transformation of being into meaning, 19, 20; transformations of interpretation, 45

undifferentiated universe, 76
unique-universal being, 80; unique and universal, 71; unique-universal human being, 81
urbanization, 72

Vico, Giambattista, 70
Vienna Circle, 52
Vorgang (Vorgang), x, 1–4, 43–44, 47–48, 50–54, 59-62, 73, 76–77, 88, 89, 100, 102, 114, 115; experience of, 1; revision of, 53; sexualization of, 49; theory of, 51

wanting, 33; two kinds, 70
Western, 115; de-Westernization, 115; Western bias, 114; Western idea, 58
word(s), 68; as the expression of thoughts, 27; as the processual means of the ineluctable, 26; in their wholeness, 26; single word, 27, 28; whole of words, 27, 28; wording, 27
world: absorbing worlds, 80; as a stage, 64, 68–69, 71, 110; transcendental, 69, 70

Yeats, William Butler, 107

Zaner, Richard M., 114
Znaniecki, Florian, 70
Zugspitze, 88, 114

About the Author

Kurt H. Wolff is Professor Emeritus of Sociology at Brandeis University. A prolific author of many books and essays, he is perhaps best known as a translator of the work of Georg Simmel and Karl Mannheim.